ASHE Higher Education Report: Volume 37, Number 4
Kelly Ward, Lisa E. Wolf-Wendel, Series Editors

Stonewall's Legacy: Bisexual, Gay, Lesbian, and Transgender Students in Higher Education

Susan B. Marine

Stonewall's Legacy: Bisexual, Gay, Lesbian, and Transgender Students in Higher Education
Susan B. Marine
ASHE Higher Education Report: Volume 37, Number 4
Kelly Ward, Lisa E. Wolf-Wendel, Series Editors

ISSN 1551-6970   electronic ISSN 1554-6306   ISBN 978-1-1181-8016-7

The ASHE Higher Education Report is part of the Jossey-Bass Higher and Adult Education Series and is published six times a year by Wiley Subscription Services, Inc., A Wiley Company, at Jossey-Bass, 989 Market Street, San Francisco, California 94103-1741.

For subscription information, see the Back Issue/Subscription Order Form in the back of this volume.

CALL FOR PROPOSALS: Prospective authors are strongly encouraged to contact Kelly Ward (kaward@wsu.edu) or Lisa Wolf-Wendel (lwolf@ku.edu). See "About the ASHE Higher Education Report Series" in the back of this volume.

Visit the Jossey-Bass Web site at **www.josseybass.com.**

The ASHE Higher Education Report is indexed in CIJE: Current Index to Journals in Education (ERIC), Current Abstracts (EBSCO), Education Index/Abstracts (H.W. Wilson), ERIC Database (Education Resources Information Center), Higher Education Abstracts (Claremont Graduate University), IBR & IBZ: International Bibliographies of Periodical Literature (K.G. Saur), and Resources in Education (ERIC).

Advisory Board

Contents

Executive Summary

In summer 1969, a riot started in the streets outside an unassuming gay bar (the Stonewall Inn), in New York City's West Greenwich Village. As the police raided the bar, a crowd of four hundred patrons gathered on the street outside and watched the officers arrest the bartender, the doorman, and a few drag queens. The crowd eventually grew to an estimated two thousand people. The next night, the crowd returned, even larger than the night before. For two hours, protesters rioted in the street outside the Stonewall Inn until the police sent a riot-control squad to disperse the crowd. The headlines the next day dismissively referred to the event as "the great faggot rebellion" (Clendinen and Nagourney, 1999, p. 23), but four decades later, this event continues to stand as the remarkable, tumultuous beginning of one of the most successful social justice movements in modern history—the movement for bisexual, gay, lesbian, and transgender (BGLT) rights in America. American higher education has been a site of both receptivity and resistance to the aims and goals of this movement, and students have been both the arbiters of change and the ground upon which this change has been wrought. Understanding the history of how BGLT students have made their way into the light on college campuses across America and what their presence means for the ways student affairs educators, faculty, and others imagine and enact higher education is the focus of this monograph.

Each chapter considers the past and present of BGLT student life from a slightly different vantage point. "Who Are BGLT College Students? A Historical Overview" sets the stage by delineating the pre- and post-Stonewall history of students on campus, from the early days of loving furtively and cautiously seeking community to the emergence of so-called "homophile leagues," the first precursors of BGLT student organizations on campus (Duberman, 1993; Katz, 1992). The slow but steady progress made by student activists to make colleges more BGLT-friendly and more responsive to their needs and concerns has changed with time. The emphases of the movement have changed from individuals seeking simple recognition to groups demanding a place at the table for deciding policies and practices with direct effects on BGLT student lives (Beemyn, 2003b; D'Emilio, 1992; Dilley, 2002a).

"Bisexual, Gay, and Lesbian Student Development Since Stonewall" reviews the beginnings and current status of what we know about student development theory as it pertains to BGLT individuals and communities in higher education. Beginning with naming the limitations of traditional student development theories, the chapter explains and explores the frameworks that focus specifically on BGLT identity, demonstrating their contributions to our understanding of how we can most effectively support BGLT young adults (Cass, 1984; D'Augelli, 1994b; Fassinger, 1998; Savin-Williams, 2001; Troiden, 1994). Over time, our understanding of the complexity of BGLT identity development has become more sophisticated, gesturing to the importance of considering students' growth and maturation through the lens of intersectionality (Abes and Jones, 2004; Abes, Jones, and McEwen, 2007; Jones and McEwen, 2000).

"Transgender Student Issues and Development After Stonewall" brings current research literature and commentary about the specific needs, concerns, and college experiences of transgender students into the conversation. Transgender students, who share diverse sexual orientations with their bisexual, gay, and lesbian peers, are a group worthy of study and advocacy in their own right. Although their stories have largely been subsumed under the umbrella of "BGLT rights," evidence suggests they experience distinct developmental paths (Devor, 2004; Morgan and Stevens, 2008). They in turn exhibit unique resiliencies, honed in response to living in environments (like most college campuses) that are hospitable to their presence. Understanding the effects of genderism (Bilodeau, 2005a, 2005b, 2007) on transgender student lives leads to important and necessary modifications to practices and policies in higher education that contribute to their sense of belonging and respect (Beemyn, 2003a, 2005; McKinney, 2005).

The establishment of a "home" in higher education has made a significant difference to many BGLT students experiencing marginality, and BGLT campus resource centers, with professional staff trained as student affairs administrators, often serve as the campus home for advancement of BGLT equity. "The BGLT Campus Resource Center" reviews the post-Stonewall foundations of BGLT campus resource centers and looks at their histories, current functions, professional staff responsibilities, and graduate training roles and responsibilities of student affairs preparation programs in dispatching effective leaders for this new profession in higher education (Sanlo, 2000; Sanlo, Rankin, and Schoenberg, 2002; Zemsky, 1996).

The final chapter provides a synopsis of one institution's recent movement toward establishing a formalized program of support for BGLT students, illustrating the utility of an approach that brings together the assets of students, faculty, and student affairs administrators in a praxis of collaborative transformation. Building on the notion that differing stakeholders' strengths and values can (and should) be meaningfully interwoven to create a full picture for improving the campus climate for BGLT people, the chapter delineates and affirms the politics of coalescence. The monograph concludes with a summary of the journey to date, with some of the remaining questions about what is next for BGLT student visibility and equity posed for the future.

Foreword

Susan B. Marine's monograph on bisexual, gay, lesbian, transgender, and queer (BGLTQ) students presents the fascinating story of how this group of college students and their needs have evolved over time. The monograph adeptly shows this evolution as a function of student activism, increasing knowledge of student development, issues raised by the emergence of the trans student community, and the increased visibility of BGLTQ centers and services on college campuses. Marine shows how these seemingly separate spheres are actually quite interrelated, demonstrating how each has influenced and shaped the other realms in different ways. She argues that much like the mainstream BGLTQ movement, higher education has been significantly transformed by those willing to be visible and public and to push boundaries: the challenge now is to continue to build support and resources that will transform higher education rather than just accommodate these students.

I found this monograph particularly interesting because I think it comes at a time when the higher education community is really trying to figure out its role in supporting students and employees who identify themselves as BGLTQ. The issues raised in the book are ones I see regularly at the University of Kansas (KU), where I work as a professor. KU recently included gender identity and gender expression in its nondiscrimination clause, but we do not yet provide full benefits to individuals who are in BGLTQ relationships. In terms of students, KU has a long history with a gay and lesbian student group. In 1970, the Gay Liberation Front, as it was initially called, saw its primary purpose as educating the university community on the nature and issues about gay people. It should be noted KU declined to formally recognize the Gay Liberation Front when it was first formed, which led to a court case initiated by the students against the university. KU won the case, but the student group was eventually recognized as an official student organization. The student group, now called Queers and Allies, is a strong, visible group on campus. It was helpful to see how other institutions have dealt with the need and concerns of these student groups and to determine in what areas places like KU need to improve and in what areas we are doing things right. It was also helpful to see how our history mirrors that of other institutions. This monograph provides needed perspective and insight into these issues.

The monograph uses a broad array of reports, studies, sources, and anecdotes in a text that is readable and engaging. Indeed, this text is currently the only one that incorporates BGLT history, administrative practices in higher education, and student development theory. Among the monograph's other strengths is the use of institutional snapshots to provide a contextual analysis of the history of BGLT student activism. Further, the section about the identity development of BGLT students provides a detailed and insightful review of BGLT-related student development theory. This section will be especially helpful to student affairs administrators and people interested in working with college-age students. The section of the monograph on intersectionality provides a thoughtful and current review of literature on multiple identities and the importance of understanding how intersecting identities can affect the experiences of BGLT college students. The transgender-focused sections add an element that is not found in other works about BGL college students.

This monograph will be useful for multiple audiences, including graduate students in student affairs or higher education programs, researchers who are interested in BGLT issues, and, most important, administrators who are looking for important links between scholarship and administrative practice. The section with recommendations at the end of the monograph is thorough and will be helpful to those individuals working directly with BGLT populations on college campuses. I hope you enjoy this monograph as much as I have.

Lisa E. Wolf-Wendel
Series Editor

Acknowledgments

First and foremost, I am deeply indebted to the pioneers of the movement for bisexual, gay, lesbian, and transgender rights, in America and around the world. When it was not socially acceptable to be BGLT, these brave and creative individuals spoke openly, organized tirelessly, and demonstrated fearlessly to ensure greater rights and more visibility in the society for BGLT people. Because of them, I am able to write and speak openly about my identity, my experiences, and my scholarly interests.

Many thanks to the editors of this series, Kelly Ward and Lisa Wolf-Wendel, and the anonymous reviewers who read and commented on this manuscript: Their insights were invaluable to my thinking. I am indebted to my former colleagues on the Working Group on BGLTQ Student Life at Harvard College, who engaged with me in a praxis of collaborative transformation that truly changed history. Finally, I give thanks to my family for their love and support and especially to my beloved partner in life, Karen Harper, whose example of intelligence and kindness is my sustenance.

Published online in Wiley Online Library
(wileyonlinelibrary.com) • DOI: 10.1002/aehe.3704

Introduction and Overview

O N THE WARM, RAINY NIGHT of September 18, 2010, at 8:42 P.M.,
Rutgers University Freshman Tyler Clementi left a note on his Facebook
wall saying that he was sorry, drove his car to the George Washington Bridge in
nearby New York City, and jumped to his death in the freezing Hudson River.
A talented concert violinist, Tyler was just becoming acclimated to his new
life in college, when he began enduring his roommate's harassment. In the
days before Tyler committed suicide, his roommate allegedly (case still pend-
ing in court) set up a Web camera in his room and secretly videotaped him
being intimate with another man. When Clementi's roommate broadcast the
video footage, the humiliation Clementi experienced overwhelmed him. In
despair, he ended his own life (Foderaro, 2010; Nutt, 2010).

Clementi's story is emblematic of the suffering endured by bisexual, gay,
lesbian, and transgender (BGLT) people, especially youth and young adults,
when they experience the aggression of intolerant others and when they feel
they cannot withstand the shame of being harassed about who they are. But
his story points to another reality: for every bit of progress that has been made
in the movement for BGLT civil rights, those with influence to do so have yet
to create an environment in American postsecondary education that is free of
mistreatment of queer individuals and communities. Thirteen years after University of Wyoming student Matthew Shepard was beaten, tied to a fence, and
left to die by two men who claimed that he had propositioned them at a local
bar (Loffreda, 2001), BGLT youth are no more immune to the violence—
emanating from others, and from within themselves—that is the by-product
of a society disdainful of sexual orientations and gender identities that stray

from the norm. More than 12 percent of the 1,195 hate crimes committed against BGLT persons in 2006 happened at schools and colleges, further demonstrating the reality that the campus is no guaranteed safe haven for queer students (Federal Bureau of Investigation, 2011).

Tyler Clementi's death is an extreme example, but other, less severe manifestations of oppression continue to surface. A young transgender man is spit on and stabbed in a bathroom at a university in California (Fishman, 2010); the door of a BGLT resident adviser is defaced in Wisconsin (Pazuniak, 2006). Members of the Westboro Baptist Church regularly picket universities across the country with their message advocating hatred and dehumanization of BGLT people (Dazio, 2011; McKee, 2010). A young man forced to consume alcohol as part of a fraternity hazing ritual lapses into a coma, and fellow members write antigay epithets on his body as he lies dying ("Anti-Gay Comments Found on Dead Pledge's Body," 2007). Senseless tragedies mingled with juvenile acts of impudence, these and other manifestations of anti-BGLT sentiment capture our attention for a fleeting moment and lend a sense of inertia to the ongoing struggle for improving campus climate for BGLT students.

But is that the whole picture of what is known about the ways that American higher education positions itself toward the BGLT student population? Although acts of aggression are far more likely than everyday victories of individual well-being and collective forward movement to garner public attention, encouraging signs are appearing as well. Colleges and universities continue to add sexual orientation, gender identity, and gender expression to their nondiscrimination policies and to recognize student groups formed to support BGLT life. Establishment and expansion of BGLT campus centers happens annually, most recently at Harvard University, where students were targeted and expelled less than a century ago for being gay (Paley, 2002a, 2002b). Individual students can, and do, thrive in American higher education, and lead in manifold ways. The professions are more open than ever before to the presence of openly BGLT leaders, including the profession of academia and higher education student affairs. What, then, explains this mixed landscape, both promising and perilous?

This book explores the progress being made on American college campuses, particularly four-year colleges and universities, through the lens of change in the time since the Stonewall riots happened in June 1969. Frequently heralded as the opening salvo in the war against oppression of BGLT people and communities, the riots coincided with a new era when queer students were emerging to claim their rightful place on campus and to advance agendas of greater recognition and acceptance. Since that time, we have come to know a great deal about the ways that BGLT students develop and grow and, accordingly, to create services and programs to empower them in their quest for belonging. It has, like the movement itself, been a gradual process of defining and refining our knowledge and in turn the policies and practices that foster belonging. It has not been a straightforward march but instead has been characterized by a persistent willingness to ask and answer vital questions about who BGLT students are and what their presence asks of us in the academy.

This monograph attempts to reveal new insights about the future of BGLT students by examining their past and by exploring how students who were once living in the shadows came to find one another and to foment campus movements. It asserts that as student affairs administrators and policymakers alike understand how young adults grow and change in their sexual orientation, gender identities, and senses of self, they can then create environments that support those changes. Examining the journeys taken by transgender and other gender-variant students as they come to grips with the realities of campuses typified by genderism (Bilodeau, 2005b) also leads to an understanding of how forward movement in these students' quest to belong has been hampered by systemic obstructions. Taking stock of the current status and future direction of BGLT campus resource centers gives a framework for thinking about the importance of community and solidarity on campus. And, finally, considering how each of these factors can be thoughtfully integrated shifts the dominant discourse from "helping BGLT students" to "transforming the campus." It is in a recommitment to this transformation that the promise of the Stonewall movement—full and complete inclusion of BGLT people in every aspect of contemporary society—can and will come full circle in the academy. And for the sake of Tyler Clementi and every other student whose safety, peace of mind, or life was taken too soon, it is an imperative we can no longer delay.

Each chapter considers the past history and present realities of BGLT student life from a slightly different vantage point, but first a note about language in this monograph.

Throughout the history of the movement to advance the rights of people who identify themselves as bisexual, gay, lesbian, and transgender, a number of different terms have been used to describe those who make up this community. Consequently, a number of different acronyms have been used as a shorthand for this community in the aggregate, each of which has interesting potentialities and limitations. The politics of which words and initials are used, and in which order, is no small matter to many who study and write on the subject of sexuality in America; indeed, according to Kulick (2000), "the coinage, dissemination, political efficacy, and affective appeal of acronyms like this deserve a study in their own right. What they point to is continued concern among sexual and gender-rights activists over which identity categories are to be named and foregrounded in their movement and their discussions. These are not trivial issues: A theme running through much gay, lesbian, and transgendered [sic] writings on language is that naming confers existence" (p. 244). Asserting one's existence through the use of naming is a deliberative act of creation, and I would be remiss as an author if I did not explain the terms I choose to use and the meaning of the order in which I use them. Throughout this monograph, I employ the initials BGLT to indicate the totality of the community about which I am writing. I use this order of letters because it is alphabetical, conveying simple English language convention rather than any particular emphasis on one (or more) of the four categories of identity.

Although it is relatively inclusive, this acronym does not in fact reflect the totality of identities subsumed under the umbrella of the community that transgresses norms of gender identity and sexual orientation; those who identify as genderqueer, transsexual, intersex, questioning, and polyamorous, who are members of the leather and bondage, dominance, and sadomasochism (BDSM) communities, and who embrace other varieties of identity are obscured in the simplistic designation BGLT. That being said, for the purposes of this book, I am writing about—and gleaning the findings of current research literature on—those who identify as bisexual, gay, lesbian, and transgender, particularly as they interface with the American higher education system as students. The research literature to date has almost exclusively focused on students who identify in these ways, indicating both a logical path for creation of this work and an open field for pursuit of further research.

Throughout the text, I also interchangeably employ the term "queer" to indicate the totality of individuals in this designation. Although not all who identify as BGLT identify as queer and in fact some vehemently object to the term (see Lauritsen, 1998), I maintain that "queer" is both a useful noun and a useful adjective to indicate one aspect of the shared nature of claiming any of these identities: that they stand apart from the "normalized" identity of heterosexual or *cisgender* individuals (cisgender, as described by Schilt and Westbrook [2009], is a term used to denote those whose assigned sex at birth generally corresponds to their gender identity and expression). Queer people are distinguishable by the ways in which their identities defy socially prescribed norms of gender identity and sexual orientation. When it is linguistically convenient, I thus employ "queer" to describe the category of those who stand outside of this norm, especially as it pertains to the case of deconstruction of normative practices and policies. Although mindful in these various ways, I also concur with Morrison's assertion (1987) that "definitions belong to the definer, not the defined" (p. 191).

When it is historically accurate to do so, I also retained the use of words like "homophile" and "homosexuality," even though such words have widely fallen out of favor for describing those who are gay or lesbian, particularly in the last decade. When the literature reviewed in this monograph opted for other combinations of letters to signify the same population studied here, such as GLBT, LGBT, or BGLTQ, I honored that use. Finally, because transgender identities are less commonly understood in the panoply of BGLT identities at this time, the words specifically associated with this identity, including cisgender, genderqueer, transgender, transsexual, and cross-dresser, are more extensively defined in "Transgender Student Issues and Development After Stonewall."

Who Are BGLT College Students?
A Historical Overview

> Homosexuality ends up at some point requiring your best thinking and effort; one's education does in fact have to be used, at crucial times.
>
> —Holleran, 1997, p. 18

A S THE TWENTY-FIRST CENTURY BEGINS, the diverse community of college students who identify as BGLT has reached new heights of visibility. Subtle shifts in the political and social value landscape, reflecting a gradual increase in awareness over the last four decades, show an increasing tolerance for gay rights; for example, 65 percent of college freshmen surveyed in 2010 supported gay marriage, compared with 58 percent of adults 18 to 29 nationwide (Lipka, 2010a). Experimentation with one's sexual orientation and gender identity, once decried by college administrators as "immoral" and "perverse" (Paley, 2002a, 2002b) is now unremarked upon at all but the most conservative campuses. Although the exact number of bisexual, gay, lesbian, and transgender students on college campuses cannot be accurately known from existing data sets, national surveys suggest that 7.2 percent of college students (American College Health Association, 2010) and 5 to 8 percent of adults aged twenty-one to ninety-four claim an identity of gay, lesbian, or bisexual (Herbenick and others, 2010); for reasons to be further explored later, it is nearly impossible to accurately know how many transgender individuals live in the United States and study in America's colleges and universities.

Although the numbers may be in dispute, recognition of the unique experiences of BGLT students is not. Narratives of openly gay students can be found in published anthologies (Howard and Stevens, 2000; Windmeyer and Freeman, 1998, 2001), in popular documentaries (Smothers, 2006; Spottiswoode, 2002), and in online social networking domains such as YouTube, Facebook, and other avenues of young adult self-expression. Gay fraternities and sororities have emerged, along with a newfound openness to welcome openly gay and lesbian students into existing mainstream fraternities and sororities (Windmeyer, 2005). In the same vein, campaigns by straight allies to make inclusive spaces for BGLT students have increased, and as of 2007, more than 3,500 gay/straight alliances have been established in American high schools for the support of BGLT adolescents (Presgraves, 2007). To date, 190 professionally staffed campus-based BGLT student centers have been founded across the country (Consortium of Higher Education LGBT Resource Professionals, 2011).

In the midst of what appears to be a positive trend of acceptance for and visibility of openly BGLT college students, more menacing realities have emerged. Hate-fueled acts of violence against BGLT young adults, most commonly symbolized by Matthew Shepard's murder in 1998 (Loffreda, 2001) and the rape and murder of Brandon Teena in 1993 (Peirce, 1999), were shocking in their brutality. The staggering cost of homophobia also drives violent urges inward; the suicides of BGLT-identified high school and college students have reached alarming proportions, as exemplified by the recent suicide of Tyler Clementi (Foderaro, 2010). Beyond the brutal anecdotes, bullying (in the form of mental, emotional, and physical abuse) is an everyday experience for many BGLT youth, as documented in numerous school climate surveys conducted by the Gay, Lesbian, and Straight Educators Network (Kosciw, Greytak, Diaz, and Bartkiewicz, 2010) and in a recent campus climate assessment conducted by Campus Pride (Rankin, Weber, Blumenfeld, and Frazer, 2010).

The dawning of the twenty-first century is thus a mixed bag in terms of what it portends for BGLT college students. Tremendous progress has been made to advance the interests of these students and to combat virulent homophobia on campus, but notable and seemingly intractable indicators of anti-BGLT oppression such as the incidents of bullying and harassment that led to Tyler Clementi's death persevere. To better understand this current moment in the evolution of students' belonging and inclusion, it is helpful to take stock of where we have been, where we are now, and where we are going. By exploring the history of BGLT college students' agency, belonging, and development, we can look to the present to examine the current state (and impact) of programs and services for BGLT students and others in the campus community and to offer predictions and recommendations about the continuing goals of progress on behalf of BGLT college students in the future. Although the interests, histories, and status of BGLT faculty, administrators, and other staff are certainly bound up in the lives and futures of students with whom they coexist, the intention of this monograph is to focus on the realities of queer college undergraduates today, specifically those at four-year colleges and universities. Where have BGLT student movements been and where are they going in terms of articulating a utopian vision of unfettered access to postsecondary education in the twenty-first century? And what will be asked of higher education as the twenty-first century progresses in terms of assuring fair, equal, and honorable treatment for these students? Through an exploration of what we know to date about BGLT students as individuals and as a group, I hope to reveal important and meaningful ways that higher education can—and must—respond to these students' developmental needs and challenges to belonging and, in so doing, maximize the potential for a more just and inclusive campus community for all.

BGLT Student History Pre-Stonewall: What Do We Know?

In the popular imagination, the history of the movement for BGLT rights began with Stonewall, the riots that took place in New York City in summer 1969. Yet ample evidence suggests that subcultures of queer life existed well before the riots, before a shared language, identity, or movement existed around which to coalesce. America's urban centers boast a particularly well-documented subculture of gay and lesbian life, dating back to precolonial times (Bullough, 2002; Chauncey, 1994; Foster, 2007). (This observation is especially true for those expressing same-sex attraction; it was more commonly documented in the period leading up to Stonewall than gender nonconformity.) Without a specific language or discernible public movement for these nonnormative attractions and expressions of gender identity, college students and other youth in the nineteenth and early twentieth centuries created unique subcultures and paved the way for a visible queer movement to emerge (Edsall, 2003).

How did same-sex attraction and gender nonconformity manifest itself on American college campuses, even before it was named? Typically, students explored same-sex desire as a function of the fact that they were living away from home, relatively unsupervised, and thus free to consider alternatives to their socially sanctioned paths. For example, women's romantic interest in other women was well documented at women's colleges from the time of their founding in the late 1800s (Faderman, 1991; Horowitz, 1984; MacKay, 1993; Zimmerman, 2003). Young women pursuing higher education at women's colleges in the early years of their founding were virtually all white women from the Northeast who were there to become better prepared for their proscribed roles as mothers and teachers.

As noted by lesbian historian Newton (2000), "As British and American women gained access to higher education and the professions, they did so in all-female institutions and in relationships with one another that were intense, passionate, and committed" (p. 178). These women were entering a social arrangement markedly different from that of other women of their era, a world without men where it was not surprising that friendship sometimes blossomed into other forms of intimacy. According to Faderman (1991), "With or without the administration's or their family's blessings, college allowed them to form a peer culture unfettered by parental dictates, to create their own hierarchy of values, and to become their own heroes and leaders, since there were no male measuring sticks around to distract, define, or detract. . . . With men living in a distant universe outside of their female world and the values of that universe suspended in favor of the new values that emerged from their new settings, young women fell in love" (pp. 19–20). Young women's resistance to the otherwise very restrictive social norms of the time found its greatest expression in close personal relationships that sometimes but not always blossomed into romantic love.

Administrators at women's colleges expressed some concern about the possibility of their students' interest in one another; euphemistically called "romantic friendship" (MacKay, 1993), these "crushes" or "smashes" were not explicitly described as sexual in nature but were often framed as a precursor to mature romantic love between women's college students and their future husbands (Inness, 1994, p. 54). Havelock Ellis (1859–1939), a British psychologist who authored the first textbook on homosexuality in 1897, warned the public of the dangers of sending a young woman to a women's college, which he described as "the great breeding ground of lesbianism" (cited in Faderman, 1991, p. 49).

How might students have witnessed their elders as they were making sense of their own feelings for other women? Women's college faculty and administrators were also often suspected of being in romantic relationships with other women, although they would not have had the luxury of being open as today's higher education leaders are. M. Carey Thomas, president of Bryn Mawr College from 1894 to 1922, was in a long-term partnership first with Mary Gwinn and later with Mary Garrett, the existence of which was well known in her campus community (Katz, 1992). Thomas once wrote that she wished "it were only possible for women to select women as well as men for a 'life's love'" and that she believed that doing so would be "one of the effects of advanced education for women" (Faderman, 1999, p. 197). In the same vein, Mount Holyoke College President Mary Woolley, who led America's oldest women's college from 1901 to 1936, lived with Jeannette Marks, a former student and faculty member (Renn, 2003). Marks, who clearly experienced conflict regarding her identity, warned her students against pursuing what she termed "abnormal friendships" with other women (Aldrich, 2006, p. 239). Still, her ardor for Woolley was undeniable, and was captured in a collection of their letters to one another throughout their fifty-two-year relationship (Wells, 1978).

Like women at women's colleges, male students who were interested in other men sexually and who attended college before Stonewall, were forging a new community and creating meaningful, if subterranean, social bonds with one another. Most of what we know about gay men's culture before Stonewall is through the memoirs of well-known public figures; Gardner Jackson, enrolling in Amherst College in 1915, encountered men's desire for other men in his fraternity, and although it was not welcome to Gardner, he was equally troubled by his classmate Robert Frost's condemnation of the practices of gay men (Katz, 1992). Poet Allan Ginsberg was a student at Columbia in the 1940s when he began to pursue romantic relationships with other male students; he was suspended for a year for allowing Jack Kerouac to sleep in his room in 1945. His feelings about his sexuality appeared to be ambivalent, as signaled by the fact that he checked himself into a mental hospital in the hopes of "curing" himself of his attraction to men (Edsall, 2003).

Though a chilly campus climate for BGLT students certainly reigned in the period before Stonewall, those whom we would now call "gay men" did find each other—and love—on campus. Ralph Waldo Emerson, entering Harvard at age fourteen in 1817, became smitten with a classmate (Martin Gay), and writing cryptically about him in his journal, seemed to be suggesting a relationship with Gay in its infancy (Katz, 1992).

Although some were able to find lively community on their campus, others' ability to locate one another—and reduce isolation—was sometimes challenging before Stonewall. Malcolm Boyd, who attended the University of Arizona in the 1940s, experienced significant emotional stress as a result of feeling isolated in his gay identity. He described his efforts to blend in: "In college, I dated for appearance's sake, and because I like to dance and be in the social company of others. I made obsessive efforts to achieve acceptable sexuality via the fraternity life. I joined the jock fraternity. I dated a number of girls, and hung my Greek pin on two or three at successive intervals" (cited in Dilley, 2002a, p. 63).

The 1950s were a particularly repressive time for BGLT students, at least in part because of the intense scrutiny being levied on gays and lesbians as part of the McCarthy-era crackdowns on anything considered "deviant" (D'Emilio, 1992). It was demonstrated in the experience of a student named Rick who entered Pomona College in 1958. Extending the isolation he experienced in high school, Rick avoided socializing, in hindsight as an effect of the fact that he perceived of his gay identity as "'a problem' that 'normal' students didn't have" (Dilley, 2002a, p. 75). For Rick and others like him in this era, imagining an active gay culture was difficult if not impossible, and, as a result, many delayed exploring their same-sex attraction until after college.

Although they might not have had a language or a public sociopolitical identity for who they were, men and women experiencing and acting on same-sex attraction, on the cusp of the revolution that was Stonewall, made efforts to create a sort of culture on campus, the epicenter of which was frequently the dramatic arts. As noted in the Oberlin College LGBT history archives, members of the theater community came to understand themselves as uniquely connected with one another by virtue of their shared interest in life as "camp"—the metaphor of life as theater (Sontag, 1966). Reflecting on his involvement in this circle in the 1960s, one gay alumnus noted, "You knew other gay people and you knew that you had a secret bond that the rest of the world didn't know about. There was an excitement, it was a little bit subversive, a little bit underworld . . . and being hidden was part of the fun. It's hard to imagine from today's perspective, but there was a real positive side to the oppression" (Plaster, 2006).

The home base of college theater played a pivotal role in enabling some queer men to discover their same-sex longings; as described by an anonymous collegian of the early 1900s, performing in an all-male musical revue as a princess, he began to notice that some of his classmates fell in love with him—and that the love endured, even after the play ended (History Project, 1998). In summary, young gay men and women in college, long before they had a shared language, visible community, resources, or any rights to speak of, were nonetheless taking considerable personal risk to express their desires and find meaningful connection with one another, setting the stage for the emergence of a revolutionary (if fledgling) movement in the next decades.

Stonewall Approaches: BGLT Visibility and Marginality in the Twentieth Century

To understand the complex balance of both the growing emergence and imposition of silence that befell those who were in same-sex relationships on college campuses before the 1960s, it is essential to understand the ways that culture operated to both support and subsume gay identity. Although having or expressing same-sex attraction during the pre-Stonewall era was not socially or culturally acceptable in a mainstream sense, a subtle cultural shift was beginning to take place. Societal mores were opening up somewhat during the progressive era (1890s to 1920s), and the early twentieth century saw a proliferation of both scientific and sociological treatises that situated same-sex desire as less a deviance than a curious cultural and biological reality. Havelock Ellis, who cautioned of the dangers of same-sex attraction between women at women's colleges, nonetheless authored what is widely considered to be the first textbook on homosexuality *(Sexual Inversion,* 1897), which affirmed homosexuality as a normal variation of adult human sexuality (Carson, 2007).

Soon after, other notable sexologists such as Magnus Hirschfeld and Karl Heinrich Ulrichs (the first to advance the idea that homosexuality was actually a "third sex" that was genetically predetermined and that those who felt same-sex attraction constituted a uniquely oppressed minority) continued to conduct research and publish on the topic of normalizing or at least countering the stigma of gay behavior and identity (Edsall, 2003). Coupled with the influence of theories advanced by Sigmund Freud that homosexuality was not ideal but also not degenerate, the work of these theorists gradually influenced the culture at large. Stopping short of making homosexuality widely acceptable, these theorists nonetheless gave a name and collectivity to those who experienced same-sex attraction, bringing their identities and interests into the light of contemporary culture. Even by those who were sympathetic to their plight, those we would now see as gay men and lesbian women, including those in college, were generally described as feeling conflicted and ashamed about their desires, which were practiced only in underground subcultures. The shame attached to these individuals' identity certainly exacted a heavy price, imposing silence that isolated them from forming visibly activist communities of support with one another until the mid-twentieth century (Duberman, 1993; Faderman, 1991).

The shame imposed on those with same-sex attraction had devastating consequences for some. Following the suicide of Cyril Wilcox (Harvard College class of 1919), a group of five deans and President A. Lawrence Lowell took action to root out a group of men in the classes of 1919, 1920, and 1921 who had been linked to activities involving same-sex relationships, parties, and links with men known to be gay in Boston. This "secret court" conducted interviews with and collected other kinds of evidence against these men, largely supplemented with testimony from Cyril Wilcox's father, branding the students' behavior as deviant and contrary to the pursuit of education. The dean stated that "the acts in question are so unspeakably gross that the intimates of those who commit these acts become tainted and . . . must for the moment be separated from the College" (Paley, 2002b). Ultimately, ten undergraduates, one graduate student, an alumnus, and a member of the faculty were dismissed from Harvard during this court's proceedings, and most were refused readmittance upon petitioning (Denizet-Lewis, 2010; Wright, 2006).

Expulsion of students believed to be gay was a commonly adopted practice among colleges in the early to mid-twentieth century and signaled a belief that homosexuality was caused by the influence of those determined to spread its ills. Newton described her own experience with this form of erasure in her essay "Too Queer for College" (2000): "Academic homophobia first struck me in college, when the Dean of Women threatened me with expulsion because I had been seen in a phone booth with another woman. We were not lovers; we had simply been talking to a mutual friend. . . . I cowered before the dean and thanked my lucky stars when she decided to accept my story. I was left in that permanent state of fearfulness and vulnerability that is the fate of those with a dirty secret" (p. 221). Thus, the mere suggestion of romantic love between two students of the same sex was considered contrary to the goals and aims of "appropriate" education during this era and could be addressed only by removing one or both of the offending parties from the environment.

Colleges and universities during this era thus viewed same-sex attraction and, more pointedly, the behaviors accompanying it, as a reflection on the institution as a whole and sought to distance themselves from it. According to Dilley (2002b), four types of institutional reactions to the presence of gay men (or men believed to be gay) were common in the era before Stonewall. Expulsions, referrals to mental health treatment as a result of viewing homosexuality as a pathology, practices of student surveillance and sting operations, and refusal to recognize student protest, speech, and organizing as legitimate typified colleges' response to claims for belonging of gay men and lesbians in the twentieth century and, in the case of curtailment of speech, continued through the late twentieth century. As a result, "nonheterosexual students' abilities to socialize, to understand themselves and their lives, and to receive an education were curtailed or negatively affected by institutional policies and procedures that neither allowed individuals who identified as nonheterosexual to be on campus nor allowed students to engage in homosexual activities, whether on or off campus. Before the 1970s, the message was clear: if a student were not heterosexual, his educational, vocational, and social opportunities—both during college and after—were at risk" (Dilley, 2002b, p. 426). As pressure mounted in reaction to the silencing, marginalization, and ostracism of students who were gay or practiced same-sex romantic and sexual attraction, it was inevitable that any movement directed toward the establishment of gay and lesbian rights would extend to America's college campuses. In the dawn of the new movement, college students, among many others, were there.

Stonewall and Its Aftermath: The Birth of the Homophile Movement

New York City, June 1969: the beginning of the Stonewall movement. Thousands of gay, lesbian, bisexual, and transgender activists filled the streets, marking the first time a collective movement of so-called "homophiles" organized against police brutality and oppression (Carter, 2004). The Stonewall riots have now been properly contextualized as the boiling point of a movement that had been building for years. Through the slow disintegration of the marchers' civil rights and the daily indignities of being labeled as "other" in a world in which normalcy was enforced with relentless ardor, the moment arrived for a large-scale act of resistance. It gestures in the same way at what is known and understood to date about BGLT college students: that their story has been gradually reassembled and amassed through the unfolding of BGLT movements on campus and students' proclivity for coalescing into one larger movement for visibility and equality.

Some evidence suggests that the first gay rights organization in the country was the Society for Human Rights, founded in Chicago in 1924, but this organization was not openly dedicated to gay rights in its charter or mission (Katz, 1992). Most historians agree that the contemporary gay rights movement in America has its most meaningful origins in the Mattachine society, the Daughters of Bilitis, and other homophile groups. The Mattachine Society, considered by most historians to be the first gay and lesbian rights organization in the United States, was founded in 1950 by Harry Hay and four other men in a desire to build group consciousness regarding a "minoritized" gay identity (Hunter, 2007a). The initiation of Mattachine dovetailed with the fervor, spearheaded by the influential (and closeted) Senator Joseph McCarthy, in identifying anything countercultural and linking it with communism. As a defensive reaction, Hay felt that he and other homosexuals (the commonly used parlance of the time) "had to organize, we had to move, we had to get started" (Katz, 1992, p. 408).

Five years later, an organization for lesbians, the Daughters of Bilitis (also known as the DOB) was founded by Phyllis Lyon and her partner, Del Martin, to incorporate women's concerns into the fight for gay rights (Gallo, 2006). Both Mattachine and the DOB had local chapters in most major American cities, and both hosted social events and political actions on behalf of the fledgling populace of openly gay people. *The Ladder*, the monthly magazine published by the DOB, brought news of the burgeoning movement to gays across America and became a beacon of new and empowering visibility. Infused with feminist values before they were mainstream, *The Ladder* and the DOB were a haven of both safety and radical thought for those seeking to liberate themselves from oppression through an explicitly lesbian feminist analysis of social conditions (Gallo, 2007).

Membership in, and visibility of, these organizations, and others like them grew steadily in the 1960s, and the political impetus for gay visibility grew more insistent as a result of widespread access to new ideologies of liberation. The civil rights movement, ushering in widespread dissent, became the proving ground for those who took up its banner—decrying racial prejudice and forging new philosophies of democratic equity. Although it is unclear whether Martin Luther King Jr.'s message of tolerance and love for one's oppressor spoke to early gay rights activists, his method of peaceful organizing and determined insistence on extension of basic civil rights to black Americans certainly resonated with organizers like those in Mattachine and the DOB, who above all sought legitimacy in their activist efforts. As King's peaceful protest vision gave way to a more active, demonstrative, and confrontational style, culminating in the civil rights March from Selma to Montgomery and the Watts riots in 1965, gay activists, many of whom were involved in the civil rights movement as college students, began to see the potential in a more active and vocal stance for their cause (Clendinen and Nagourney, 1999; Katz, 1992).

Feminism, too, informed the evolution of the gay rights movement and enlarged the discourses available to gay rights activists. The second wave of feminism, beginning in the early 1960s with the publication of Betty Friedan's *The Feminine Mystique* (1963), was typified by the practice of consciousness raising. Small groups of women came together to share personal insights into the nature of their lives, weaving together explanations of their oppression that resonated across age, class, and, to a more limited extent, differences in race and sexuality. Although it is often critiqued as a social movement mostly geared to the interests and concerns of white middle-class women, second-wave feminism was, for many, a period of intense awakening about their same-sex desires for other women. Feminism's relationship to lesbianism was not seamless; in fact, many experienced discrimination in the movement as they sought to advance their interests and equality. Radical lesbian feminists, who later embraced the term to signify their defiant exodus from the isolation they experienced in mainstream feminist movements, were derisively characterized by leaders of the movement as the "lavender menace" (Duberman, 1993; Jay, 1999).

While Mattachine, the DOB, and other gay identity groups continued to build a base of support from those who wanted a more mainstream form of social progress, tension emerged from others—mostly young and heavily identified with the civil rights, antiwar, and feminist movements—who began to stake a claim for their own form of radical activism. On the heels of the Stonewall riots, these activists emerged to claim a new space for organizing, rejecting the "go along to get along" tactics of their forebears (Katz, 1992). The Gay Liberation Front (GLF), founded several weeks after the Stonewall riots by those impatient with the state of gay liberation activism, was led by Jim Fouratt, Martha Shelley, and other defectors from the Mattachine Society and the DOB chapters in New York City (Kardia, 2007). The GLF became the new vanguard of the movement, with outposts in Berkeley, Chicago, Philadelphia, Los Angeles, Paris, and Sydney; its most active chapter overseas comprised radical activist students from the London School of Economics (Power, 1995). Even as they operated with Marxist political practices like consensus-driven meeting structures and nonhierarchical leadership, these organizations, like their predecessors, were typified by the concerns of white, middle class, affluent gay men and, as a result, splintered within two years as women, gay activists of color, and radical lesbian feminists sought to create their own communities (Clendinen and Nagourney, 1999).

Far from being a smooth evolution, this fragmentation was often accompanied by painful recognition of the limits of a "one-face" movement. Signaling her departure in 1970 from organized gay rights activism, Del Martin declared, "goodbye to the male chauvinists of the homophile movement who are so wrapped up in the 'cause' that they lose sight of the people for whom the cause came into being. . . . 'Gay is good,' but not good enough—so long as it is limited to white males only" (Clendinen and Nagourney, 1999, p. 95). Nearly half a century later, historians agree that although women of all races, gays and lesbians of color, and transgender and other gender-nonconforming people of all races were active and present in the emerging movement for gay rights, their identities and concerns were often subsumed by white gay men of means, leaving an incomplete record of their contributions and an overwhelming sense of their individual and collective marginalization in the historical record (Carter, 2004; Clendinen and Nagourney, 1999; Duberman, 1993; Jay, 1999; Katz, 1992).

Transgender Lives and Stonewall

The Stonewall riots were a time of rapid escalation of visibility for many in the BGLT community. Perhaps none were more vital to the burgeoning movement (yet less recognized) than transgender individuals. Cross-dressers, transsexuals, and others who are part of the umbrella of transgender identity were deeply woven through the cultural fabric of late 1960s New York, and although not yet understood as a distinct group from those who identify as gay, lesbian, or bisexual, their leadership was integral to the crescendo of activism in summer 1969 (Carter, 2004; Duberman, 1993). In a similar fashion, the activism of transgender youth was a pivotal force in what is largely seen to be the precursor to Stonewall, the uprising at Compton's Cafeteria in San Francisco in 1966 (Highleyman, 2007b). Sylvia Rivera, a leading community figure in the East Village, was a Puerto Rican/Venezuelan transsexual activist whose commanding presence and decisiveness about fighting police brutality resonated with others at the riots, wrought with a sensibility she developed after surviving significant sexual and physical violence while in jail (Clendinen and Nagourney, 1999; Duberman, 1993). Foregrounding the stories of young gay men in place of the less socially visible transactivist like Rivera, historians generally played down her role in the riots or ignored it altogether until Duberman (1993) resurrected her narrative in the early 1990s. This omission symbolizes the tendency of documented queer history to marginalize transcontributions to the movement, in a practice Stryker (2008) refers to as "homonormativity." The result was that for many years, people thought of Stonewall as a gay rebellion: as noted by Gan (2007), "published news accounts, for mainstream as well as gay publications, generally elided the roles of gender-variant people and people of color at Stonewall, while subsuming them under the term 'gay'" (p. 132).

Today, the centrality of Rivera's contribution to the struggle for transgender justice in and through moments like Stonewall is memorialized through the name of the leading legal advocacy organization for transgender people in the United States—the Sylvia Rivera Law Project (2011). And although the evolving effort to support, understand, and advocate for gay, lesbian, and bisexual college students has come to include transgender individuals as well, the limited literature on this student population to date suggests that much work to advocate effectively for the needs of transgender college students remains.

BGLT Rights on the College Campus: The Student Homophile Movement

While the BGLT rights movement history was being hashed out in the major urban areas across America, a parallel and sometimes intertwined movement for gay liberation on American college campuses was also coming to voice in the late 1960s. It is important to note that student organizing, even for the benign goal of forming community among isolated individuals, was strongly opposed in many circles of academe; administrators had refused to recognize BGLT student groups, perceiving that doing so "would not be beneficial to the normal development of [the institution's] students" (Bayer, 1981, p. 119).

Nevertheless, as the breakthrough moment for the BGLT resistance movement neared, the first chapter of the Student Homophile League (or SHL, later called "Gay People at Columbia-Barnard") was founded at Columbia University in 1967 by an openly bisexual student named Stephen Donaldson, aka Robert Martin. (It was common practice in the early years of the gay rights movement that leaders and "foot soldiers" alike chose pseudonyms for safety.) Calling the group "a vehicle for students of all orientations to combat homophobia" (Highleyman, 2007a, p. 172), the group struggled to gain official recognition from the administration; Donaldson eased the anxiety of administrators at Columbia by submitting a list of members that included "big men on campus" (Dynes, 2002, p. 269). Their activities included organizing lectures, integrating school-sponsored dances, and offering counseling to students struggling with their sexuality.

One challenge the group faced was to discern a way to be identifiable to those seeking membership when most were not themselves "out"; as Donaldson lamented when interviewed by *The New York Times*, "We have to figure out some way of interviewing persons who say they want to become members" (Schumach, 1967, p. 1). The group also took on the medical establishment in 1968, storming a panel discussion of physicians known to pathologize gay identity and demanding they rescind their condemnation of gay behavior, instead positioning gay individuals as an oppressed minority group (Duberman, 1993). Donaldson later described this event as the "first gay demonstration in New York City," predating Stonewall by more than a year (Donaldson, 1992, p. 261). (Notably, Donaldson was involved in a brief affair with Martha Shelley, one-time president of the Daughters of Bilitis in New York, a vivid example of the ways that nonheterosexual identity in this era was flexible and relative.)

The SHL formed chapters, loosely knit into a cross-state collaborative, at other campuses in the years following Stonewall, including Cornell and New York Universities (Teal, 1971). Regarding the genesis of the Cornell chapter's activism, Beemyn (2003b) found that the SHL was comprised of both openly gay and heterosexual students, that it was formed as both a political and social organization, and that its members participated in a successful and visible 1969 campaign in alliance with black students to protest the administration's insensitivity to their needs. Once the leadership got a taste of the potential successes of radical organizing, the SHL moved away from its assimilationist roots and toward a new vision of queer liberation. Eschewing the original name to reflect the redefined, coalition-based consciousness, the SHL at Cornell became the Cornell Gay Liberation Front (GLF), and members began dropping pseudonyms and claiming their membership proudly and publicly. As Beemyn (2003b) noted, "By discussing their lives in front of various audiences and countering the stereotypes of lesbians, gay men, and bisexuals, they and subsequent groups at other colleges helped make it possible for many more gay people to accept themselves and come out" (p. 223).

Students advocating for acceptance of BGLT identities also mobilized in this era to create dedicated campus spaces for coalescing. The oldest gay and lesbian student center on record, the Queer Student Cultural Center (previously named "fight repression of erotic expression," or FREE) was founded in May 1969, nearly two months before the Stonewall riots, at the University of Minnesota (Wehrwein, 1969). One of its founders, Jack Baker, was the first openly gay man to become student body president at a major university as well as the first person to sue for marriage rights in his state of residence ("Adopting a Lover," 1971).

Signaling a shift toward a bolder, more radical stance regarding the terms of liberation, students at the City College of New York chose the name HI! (standing for "homosexuals intransigent") and became the first campus organization to embrace the word "homosexual" in its name. Group founder Craig Schoonmaker noted, "We think the word 'homophile' is a stupid, cowardly euphemism. . . . We see nothing wrong with the word 'homosexual.' Besides, homophile is intended to give leeway for heterosexuals to participate in the movement. But we think the drive for homosexual self-respect is primarily a homosexual responsibility; indeed, it can only be accomplished by homosexuals" (Teal, 1971, p. 45). His mission was explicit support of the LGBT undergraduate and declared its intention to "instill self-affirming attitudes in students who have recently discovered themselves to be homosexually oriented" (Teal, 1971, p. 44).

Student Movement Snapshots: BGLT Student Activism at Three Institutions

Student movements for BGLT rights proliferated at campuses around the country in the 1970s following Stonewall, generated by persistent, creative organizers using methods and approaches borrowed from successful student movements for black civil rights and feminist organizing. Steeped in the continuing belief that same-sex attraction and nonnormative gender expression was marked by deviance, administrators were not uniformly keen on recognizing these groups. Their success often depended on partnerships between determined students and sympathetic or allied faculty and administrators. D'Augelli (1989), in his study of the movement for recognition of the BGLT student organization at Pennsylvania State University in the 1970s, observed that "just as the power of a dean's tribunal was used to define lesbian and gay life as antithetical to campus life, so too can academic leaders use their moral authority to acknowledge lesbians and gay men as equal citizens of an academic community" (p. 128).

The impetus for students to take up the mantle of equality on their respective campuses has been largely motivated by necessity and has led to both crushing failure and resounding success. As student movements on campus formed, reformed, and evolved, their mission and purpose became increasingly inclusive and expansive. Nonheterosexual students on campus were gaining not only local but national momentum: as noted in *The New York Times* in 1970, "In defiance of taboos, thousands of college students are proclaiming their homosexuality and openly organizing 'gay' groups on large and small campuses across the country. No one knows exactly how many are involved, but in growing numbers they are forming cohesive organizations . . . and [making] substantial strides in changing attitudes" (Reinhold, 1971). To better understand the contours of these evolutions, three snapshots of student movements on campus for BGLT rights—at Oberlin College, Penn State University, and Cornell University—are explored.

Oberlin College

Oberlin, a liberal arts college of 2,800 located in northwest Ohio has a colorful and progressive history marked by its proud claim to being the first institution to enroll black students in a racially integrated environment (in 1835) and to admit women in a coeducational environment (in 1841). Under the motto "learning and labor," students at Oberlin study traditional liberal arts subjects or attend the institution for its highly selective conservatory of music. Oberlin's long history of political progressivism is reflected in its BGLT student history; its first queer student organization, Oberlin Gay Liberation (OGL), was founded in 1971 (Plaster, 2006). Approximately forty students gathered in a classroom building to discuss the formation of a student group to advocate for what were described as mostly personal needs, including counseling and support, and declared openness of agenda and participation by all, regardless of "sexual preferences" (Ecksmith, 1971).

A few weeks later, an editorial in *The Oberlin Review* by African American student John E. Adams (1971) signaled the connections some students were making between liberation for those who were gay and other social justice movements. Adams wrote, "Homosexuality, like Women's Liberation, allows us to reject all the dehumanizing masculine/feminine roles this society forces on people, and to build new ways of relating to each other as equal human beings. It allows us to examine, and to reject, the whole nuclear family structure, which locks woman to man, and children to both, in a box that limits human growth and perpetuates the authoritarian, male-dominated model of human relationships" (p. 6).

Reminding readers that this "new" ideology of Gay Lib is "not only an organization, it is a MOVEMENT," Adams called on other students to join in the process of creating a better life for future gay students at Oberlin (Adams, 1971, p. 6). The founders of the OGL advocated for "[seeking] freedom of sexual expression and an end to sexist oppression of gay people . . . , [eliminating] the harassment of gay people as evidenced by open hostility and by covert sexist attitudes, . . . [and helping] gay people have an open and full sex life by sponsoring social events" (Oberlin College archives, cited in Plaster, 2006). The group experienced resistance from the administration in its initial efforts to be recognized but ultimately had the charter approved in September

1971. Despite its members' advocacy for radical social change on a variety of fronts related to racial, national, and gender oppression, the group was primarily social in focus. Integrating dances to include visible same-sex couples and reducing internalized homophobia became the primary activities of the OGL in its early years (Plaster, 2006).

Within a few years of its founding, the OGL became the Oberlin Gay Union, focusing more on unifying Oberlin's BGLT community than asserting radical change: the mission statement emphasized the group's efforts to "meet the social, emotional, personal, educational, and political needs of people in the gay community" and to "promote interaction and communication between the gay and other communities" (Plaster, 2006). Embracing the banner of queer identity, the current reformation of the group is known as Oberlin College Lambda Union and cites its mission as "providing a forum for the political, social, emotional, and educational needs of lesbian, gay, bisexual, transgender, transsexual, queer and questioning people and their allies in the Oberlin community. By organizing and funding various political, educational and social events, Lambda tries to advance understanding and respect not only between queer and non-queer people, but also between the many fragments of the greater queer community" (Oberlin College Lambda Union, 2011).

Oberlin College stands as a shining example of BGLT student activism in the 1970s, a time when many would consider middle America to have been behind the curve on gay visibility. But assumptions about where politically active BGLT youth congregate and foment change are not always accurate, as is vividly shown in the next example of BGLT student activism, in State College, Pennsylvania.

Pennsylvania State University

Pennsylvania State University, a large rural land-grant institution in central Pennsylvania, is an example of the slow and steady burn that can erupt in student movements, just as it did with Stonewall. As the result of an important confluence of events, Penn State's bucolic campus became the site of a small but meaningful student protest in 1992, when approximately thirty members of the lesbian, gay, and bisexual student alliance joined together to declare pride in their identities as part of National Coming Out Day. This event was the culmination of two decades of persistent, sustained activism on the part of BGLT activists at the university, who had been resisting marginalization since Penn State officials denied them recognition in 1971 as the Homophiles of Penn State (D'Augelli, 1989). Working quietly and consistently to urge the institution to include sexual orientation in its stated nondiscrimination policy, these activists took a courageous stand for equality of sexual identity. In 1985, Penn State students organized further to demand a group for support of students, advised by noted developmental theorist Anthony D'Augelli (whose work is further explored in the next chapter), who noted that college students "are at a critical age when they start to come to terms with some of their feelings. . . . They end up doing a lot of things to maintain . . . secrecy, which takes a lot of energy" (McCauley, 1985, p. 5). Creation of a safe haven for students where this secrecy could be reduced was an essential component of student community building in this era; the courage of student activists who went on record as the publicly identified point people for such organizations is indeed remarkable.

Particularly in a conservative area such as central Pennsylvania, this movement proved to be no small feat: death threats levied at gay students and counterprotests by conservative students created a backdrop of hostility that made any such activism a truly brave endeavor (Rhoads, 1998). Ultimately, facing the possibility of a student takeover of the president's office, the Penn State board of trustees approved the addition of sexual orientation to the nondiscrimination policy in 1992. Penn State's nondiscrimination policy was put to the test in 2006 when a student claimed the women's basketball coach, Rene Portland, had removed her from the team for being a lesbian. The university conducted its own investigation into the matter, found that Portland created a hostile environment for players, and levied a fine of $10,000 (DiPerna, 2006).

In 2011, a "pride parade" through campus attended by nearly two hundred people (Gallagher, 2011) demonstrated the growth in visibility that is possible when institutions commit to enacting policies and practices that affirm the equality of BGLT students.

Cornell University

The Ivy League, a loosely knit group of eight of America's most selective colleges and universities, is the site of many important cultural and social shifts, and the persistently student-generated movement for BGLT rights is certainly among them. One notable example is the gradual and steady movement for advancement of the status of BGLT students (and others) at Cornell University (founded in 1865 in Ithaca, New York). Not that it was always so: Ellen Coit Brown recalled that a female classmate in the 1880s was expelled from Cornell for attending a concert in town with another female student, who was dressed as a man (Katz, 1992), then reinstated later with no trace of the "male" suitor.

When an alumna declared Yale "the gay Ivy" in a *Wall Street Journal* article in 1987, she was not giving due credit to the Ivy that had the first student homophile group—Cornell. A closer look at Cornell's history of increasing BGLT inclusivity reveals some of the same fault lines as other colleges—and the importance of student activism for changing the terms of the debate. Cornell's BGLT student organization, a branch of the Student Homophile League founded at Columbia, was chartered as an official student organization in March 1968 without submitting the names of its members for privacy reasons. In this case, the group was chartered before a meeting occurred in November of that same year. The group's early activities included lectures featuring noted gay scholars Frank Kameny and Barbara Gittings and soon commenced printing a newsletter and running a gay night at a local bar. A month of educational activities, once called May Gay and now called Gaypril, also became a mainstay of the group's community-building emphasis (McCray and Marston, 1991).

Like other student BGLT affinity groups in the wake of Stonewall, the SHL at Cornell went through an interesting transition of name and purpose in 1970, when it began referring to itself as the Gay Liberation Front, in closer alignment with the goals and politics of the women's movement. A stronger activist bent, including a focus on overturning state sodomy prohibitions as well as laws banning "homosexual loitering," was taken up, and student leaders involved in these efforts were more willing to self-identify as members of record ("Student Homophile League Now 'Gay Liberation Front,'" 1970). Around this time, the group became politicized when the owner of the bar that many BGLT students frequented stated publicly that he "didn't like homosexuals": in a Stonewall-esque show of solidarity, students from the Gay

Liberation Front showed up en masse to occupy the bar, insisting on being respected as patrons. When the members arrived, the bar's owner blocked the doors, stating that the establishment was closed for the night and resulting in a call by the GLF for Cornell students to boycott the discriminatory tavern ("Boycott Morrie's," 1970).

At least partly in reaction to the chilly reception they received in the local community, a Gay People's Center was founded on the campus in the third year of the group's operation, funded jointly by the university and by the student government, providing a safe home base for the group's activities. Symbolizing a move away from a "gay ambassador" emphasis, one student leader told *The Cornell Daily Sun* that the GLF's original purpose was educational but that "I've become convinced that our energies are better spent helping ourselves" (Brenner, 1972, p. 7). Eventually, the pendulum swung back toward a balance of developing both a communal and a political emphasis. A dance held in 1974 attracted 220 people "as well as five unsolicited streakers from the nearby Delta Upsilon fifties party," denoting some students' perceptions of BGLT students' social life as worthy of mockery (Calhoun, 1974, p. 6).

In keeping with the national movement in the late 1970s to establish programs of study about queer history, identity, and politics, BGLT students at Cornell began to advocate for the establishment of a gay studies course, inviting faculty from nearby Ithaca College (where gay studies was already in the curriculum) to help them strategize. Encountering both support and resistance from faculty to whom they brought the idea, the students wondered about the plausibility of finding a departmental "home" such as in sociology, anthropology, women's studies, or political science. Two of the greatest advocates for the notion, pioneering sex roles researchers Sandra and Daryl Bem, concurred with the course's usefulness, while the director of freshman seminars at Cornell stated that a course on homosexuality was not "emotionally plausible" and could be a "frightening" topic for a freshman-level course ("University Profs Show Little Interest in Establishing Gay Course at Cornell," 1980).

Unlike other student BGLT movements of the immediate post-Stonewall era, the Cornell BGLT student group appeared to enjoy consistent, if modest, support from the institution itself and thus mobilized more of its energy toward combating negative reactions from peers and the community than the administration. Like many communities, the strength, numbers, and visibility of Cornell BGLT student activism waxed and waned over the years but continues to thrive as Direct Action to Stop Heterosexism, along with a transgender advocacy committee, a graduate and professional student LGBTQ collective, and an umbrella group, the Haven, that unites these and other student, faculty, and staff initiatives (Cornell University Lesbian, Gay, Bisexual, and Transgender Resource Center, 2011).

Queer Student Activism Today

As these three institutional snapshots show, BGLT students after Stonewall employed varied and meaningful approaches to transforming their campus communities. The groups morphed themselves from purely social or support-based entities to formidable voices for change, on campus and in the community beyond. They forged new styles of leadership, grappled with questions of solidarity and fragmentation, and often had to contend with a campus community that was apathetic, if not hostile, to their existence. Still, they persevered and in most cases, their reach and stability continued to expand with each passing year.

What about BGLT student activists today? What do we know of their leadership, and what are the continuing strands of purpose, belief, or practice that these groups have inherited from their Stonewall-era forebears? Scanning the headlines might lead one to believe that social protest is dormant, if not dead, at most colleges and universities in America, especially when compared with the powder-keg atmosphere of the 1970s. But as noted by Rhoads (1998), student volunteerism and social change movements steadily, if less visibly, increased in the late twentieth century, fueled by students' sharpening awareness of the mechanisms of power that served to disenfranchise. According to the Higher Education Research Institute, only 6 percent of students indicate that they plan to participate in student demonstrations while in college (though 26.2 percent did so in high school), while 30.8 percent plan to take part in community service or volunteerism, indicating a greater commitment to social change than social protest (*Chronicle of Higher Education Almanac,* 2010). Given these factors, it follows logically that student activism centered on sexual orientation and gender identity has become less frequent and volatile while at the same time becoming more focused.

Research on BGLT campus activists, while limited, offers some insight into their priorities and objectives. In one study, gay men appear to be less confident than lesbian women about their leadership abilities in contexts where non-BGLT students operate (Porter, 1998). Renn and Bilodeau (2005a, 2005b) found that participation in student leadership in BGLT activism mirrored certain aspects of D'Augelli's life span model of BGLT identity development and not only helped student leaders build a sense of self-efficacy but also accelerated students' process of coming out to self, family, and the campus. Sustained involvement in BGLT student leadership as a conference planner also encouraged connection with others in the BGLT student community and ushered in a more interwoven experience of their BGLT identity development. Renn (2007) also found that BGLT students' degree of "outness" also appears to be positively correlated to involvement in leadership activities and that time and energy invested in activities related to one's BGLT identity took shape in one of three ways. Students in this study identified as an LGBT student leader (working within the system and "doing" leadership), as an LGBT student activist (whose leadership style was more transformational in nature and did not depend on positional roles), or as a queer activist (motivated by deconstructing and dismantling power across different dimensions of oppression). Careful not to identify one typology as inherently superior, Renn affirmed that many forms of campus activism and leadership on BGLT issues are valuable and that "campuses need social, political, and educational activities related to a number of historically marginalized groups" (Renn, 2007, p. 327).

Although BGLT students often conduct activism in campus environments rife with a multitude of climate, safety, and inclusiveness obstacles, pragmatism dictates that activists must have focus. BGLT student activists today have typically directed their energies internally to change in their institutions, continuing the struggle for a more BGLT-inclusive campus and for a stronger commitment to cohesion between the institution's stated values and practice. In their own campus domains, student activists' work today centers on three types of change: increasing tolerance for BGLT life at religiously focused institutions, expanding gender-neutral housing to better accommodate the needs of gender-variant students, and questioning the legitimacy of the presence of the American military's branch on campus, the Reserve Officer Training Corps.

BGLT Visibility in Religiously Affiliated Colleges

Students at religiously affiliated institutions face a number of challenges navigating a campus environment that typically casts same-sex attraction and relationships and nonnormative gender identity and expression as counter to the teachings of the faith, particularly at Catholic, evangelical Christian, and Orthodox Jewish institutions. Many of these institutions have, and enforce, student codes of conduct that prohibit same-sex relationships. Administrators, fueled by the support of the leadership of their respective denominations and alumni, have actively blocked the recognition of BGLT students and movements at American institutions associated with more conservative sects of Christianity and Orthodox Judaism (Mooney, 1994; Smith, 2007). Institutions with religious affiliations routinely invoke history, mission, and core values in an effort to stigmatize BGLT identity, visibility, and sense of belonging (Levine and Love, 2000).

Religiously conservative colleges' leadership has argued that BGLT groups are incompatible with institutional doctrine, and although allowing students to organize under the principles of freedom of association, they typically withhold recognition and support of such activities. In some instances, individual students have been suspended or expelled from religiously affiliated colleges when their gay identity has been discovered (Hoover, 2006; Kellogg, 2001). Students at conservative historically black colleges and universities (HBCUs) have also suffered the double marginality frequently noted by black gay activists and scholars, explained away by the notion that homosexuality is a threat to the black family in America (Walker, 2007). In response to student activism, some HBCUs are moving toward more progressive policies, including the addition of sexual orientation to existing nondiscrimination policies (Oguntoyinbo, 2009).

The kind of marginalization and erasure these strictures impose is untenable to BGLT activists at these institutions, who adopt a variety of strategies to make themselves visible, including advancing a presence for queer students on the Internet (Harding University Queer Press, 2011) and continuing to operate student support groups without recognition or endorsement, in violation of these prohibitions (Eckholm, 2011; Friess, 2007). To compound the efforts of on-the-ground leaders, a national student movement, Soulforce (2011), charters buses with activist volunteers to visit BGLT-unfriendly colleges in the hope of changing their minds and policies through their commitment to nonviolent social action. Although their tactics are nonconfrontational and emphasize dialogue, the movement's members have been arrested on several campuses for trespassing (Nelson and Cloyd, 2006; Smith, 2007). Activists' efforts to formalize a BGLT student identity at religious institutions typically raise questions about the line between institutional autonomy and freedom of expression and frequently become the subject of litigation—a powerful symbol of student activists' effectiveness (National On-Campus Report, 2006).

Activism for Gender-Neutral Housing

Not specific to institutions with strong faith traditions, a second issue that is mobilizing BGLT students (and their allies) across America is the increasing awareness of the limitations of traditional housing policies and practices, particularly for transgender and other gender-nonconforming students. Same-sex housing assignments impose limitations on students and require them to conform in a binary system that does not recognize their gender identity or expression. Although the first activists proposing agendas of gender neutrality attended northeastern liberal private colleges like Wesleyan ("Wesleyan Gets Beyond Gender," 2003) and Swarthmore (Borrego, 2001), student activists at public universities like Michigan and the University of California system have also recently ushered in changes, questioning not only the forced choice mandated by same-gender housing but also the presumption of students' heterosexuality of traditional housing assignment procedures (Marklein, 2004). Housing assignment processes are one of many structural impediments to full inclusion of transgender students; students have taken actions to press for greater inclusion on all fronts, including designation of gender-neutral bathrooms, gender-inclusive applications and other forms, and the ability to change one's sex and preferred name in official record-keeping mechanisms (Tilsley, 2010).

Activism Around the Presence of ROTC

A third site of activist movement that BGLT students have fomented in recent years regards the presence of ROTC, the military's reserve officer training corps, on campus. Until the December 2010 congressional action (H.R. 2965) to overturn the don't ask, don't tell policy, which mandated that bisexual, gay, and lesbian service members must conceal their sexual orientation from public knowledge while enlisted, all members of the armed services (including students participating in Reserve Officer Training Corps programs) were forced to comply (Steinhauer, 2010). Once opposed because it symbolized a promilitary agenda, the ROTC now was the target of those who recognized the hypocrisy their institutions practiced by having an active ROTC unit on campus. Students correctly inferred that such programs, if instituted at universities with nondiscrimination policies inclusive of sexual orientation and gender identity/expression, would be in violation of these policies and thus took action to question the ROTC's presence (French, 2009; "New ROTC Unit Protested at University," 2008). On some campuses where ROTC has been reinstated, BGLT student activists and their allies continue to question the military's discriminatory stance against transgender and other gender-non-conforming members and the choices made by their institutions' leadership even in the face of this glaring inconsistency ("Agreement Allows the ROTC to Return to Harvard After Decades Away," 2011; "Harvard Ends Four-Decade Ban on ROTC, Yale Next," 2011).

Conclusion: BGLT Student Visibility and Activism After Stonewall

In the four decades that have passed since Stonewall, BGLT activist endeavors today have moved away from a debate about their right to be, shifting the focus to transforming institutions to be more welcoming, to enable greater visibility of BGLT student causes and concerns and to hold institutions accountable for consistency in policy and practice. Although student movements on campus to advance BGLT rights have gained greater visibility and prominence, some students continue to feel marginalized in the context of these groups. Bisexual students are among them. Groups such as Bisexuals Talk and Eat (BiTE) at Brown University and Fluid at the University of California at Los Angeles have formed to address the specific needs of bisexual-identified students and to minimize the judgment and skepticism they encounter in groups primarily formed (tacitly) to serve lesbian and gay students (Morgan, 2002). Similarly, transgender students often experience marginalization in queer organizing on campus, requiring them to splinter into their own groups, where they may be less supported and visible (Smothers, 2006; Tilsley, 2010).

As illustrated in this chapter, American college students who identify as bisexual, gay, lesbian, or transgender have made tremendous strides over the last century in advancing the cause of inclusion and belonging on the college campus—and have transformed the campus with their presence and persistent voice. Not content to simply be, many activists have worked to "queer" the campus—to transform the way that sexual orientation and gender identity are understood and imagined. Faculty, staff, alumni, and alumnae have been part of this forward movement, but we cannot and must not underestimate the impact of student agitation. In a lecture given at Oberlin College reflecting on the state of higher education's friendliness to queer life in the early 1990s, D'Emilio (1992) observed that "until now, gay and lesbian students"—and I would add, bisexual and transgender activists as well—"have contributed the most to the quest for equality. It is admirable, and not surprising, that they have done so, but they should not have to carry this responsibility forever" (p. 135). As the twenty-first century begins and student activists continue to carry forward the mantle of progress, it remains to be seen whether they will be alone or accompanied in that work.

Bisexual, Gay, and Lesbian Student Development Since Stonewall

> We have to change how everyone understands the range of sexual identities and gender identities. . . . It's more than just gay and straight, men and women, Black and White, you know?
>
> —BGLT student activist, in Renn, 2007, p. 325

EXPERIMENTATION, GROWTH, AND CHANGE are the cornerstones of the college experience. College students, particularly those of traditional age, undergo a myriad of personal, intellectual, and interpersonal adjustments during their college years, which have been well documented in scholarly research (Arnold and King, 1997; Evans and others, 2010; Pascarella and Terenzini, 2005). The need to better understand college student development was initially largely pragmatic; following two tumultuous World Wars, colleges were teeming with young people with interests and aptitudes that needed to be matched to an ideal vocation (Evans and others, 2010).

The college guidance movement, which morphed into the student personnel movement, set about researching and documenting the paths of students, including their "intellectual capacity and achievement, [their] emotional makeup, [their] physical condition, [their] social relationships, [their] vocational aptitudes and skills, [their] moral resources, [their] economic resources, and [their] aesthetic appreciations" (American Council on Education, 1937). Implicit in this holistic focus on the developing student, but not explicitly stated, was the growing acknowledgment that students' personal and intimate lives matter in who they are becoming and play a large role in the shaping of their self-concepts as adults. The theoretical foundation of the student personnel movement, student development theory, has historically presumed a degree of universality about young adult human development, change, and growth in personality and social and relational experience and has relied on this presumption in the training and development of new professionals.

The theorists whose work predominates the student development theory literature, such as Arthur Chickering (1969), William Perry (1970), and Lawrence Kohlberg (1971), conducted research at a time when students' gender identity was perceived of in fixed binary terms, male or female, and their sexual orientation was uniformly perceived as heterosexual. Since that time, many scholars have debated the universal applicability of theories developed while operating under these assumptions with subject pools comprising almost entirely privileged white males (Belenky, Clinchy, Goldberger and Tarule, 1986; Cross, 1971; Gilligan, 1982; Helms, 1990; Wall and Evans, 2000). From different disciplinary perspectives, these theorists have cogently argued that differences of gender, race, and sexual orientation have significant impact on students' experiences and sense of place on the college campus (and in the world at large). That we can no longer presume a "universal student" means that our understanding of students' self-defined perspectives and positions must be honored.

Before the Stonewall era, it would have been nearly unthinkable to conceive of bisexual, gay, lesbian, and transgender students as a uniquely developing group of individuals. BGLT students during this era certainly attended college (Dilley, 2002a; MacKay, 1993), yet the expression of their sexuality and gender identities was not considered normal or desirable and instead would have been considered "abnormal" in their development, owing to the standards of the day (Dynes, 1990; Feinberg, 1996; Garnets and Kimmel, 1993; Lewis, 2010). Alfred Kinsey's seminal work (1948; see also Institute for Sex Research, 1953), showing that as many as 4 percent of men and 3 percent of women were exclusively homosexual and that 37 percent of men and 28 percent of women had had some sexual experience with a person of their own sex, did not take hold in the public consciousness to shift the debate about sexual "normalcy" until much later. Kinsey's work and the effort to understand gay individuals as something other than abnormal was amplified by the research of Evelyn Hooker. A behavioral psychologist, Hooker (1961) studied the personalities, habits, and adjustment of gay men and, when comparing them with heterosexual men, found no significant differences.

While scientists like Kinsey and Hooker were arguing for a more expansive vision of sexuality, the medical establishment continued to hold fast to the view that homosexuality and "disorders" of gender identity were pathologies, characterized by maladjustment and stress, and not to be encouraged or supported in healthy adults (American Psychiatric Association, 1952, 1968). This perspective—at least as it pertained to sexual orientation—changed rapidly following Stonewall, and as the 1970s began, activists inside and outside the medical community lobbied successfully for the removal of homosexuality from the *Diagnostic and Statistical Manual of Mental Disorders* of the American Psychiatric Association (Pope, 2007; Stoller and others, 1973). Although homosexuality is no longer included in the list of recognized mental illnesses treated by modern psychiatry, the continued inclusion of so-called gender identity disorders (American Psychiatric Association, 2000) serves to pathologize transgender and other gender-variant people, resulting in marginalization and discrimination against these communities (discussed further in the next chapter).

As the social and cultural changes brought to the fore following Stonewall slowly shifted the psychological profession's view of sexual development, so too did we begin to understand the evolution of sexual orientation in a different, more positive way—and could begin to envision what the college experience meant for those who are making sense of themselves as bisexual, gay, or lesbian.

Bisexual, Gay, and Lesbian Identity Development

How do we understand, and help them to understand, students' emerging identities as bisexual, gay, or lesbian? Sorting out the pieces of this puzzle can vary tremendously according to an individual's context, background, and access to information, support, and other resources. Before the last decade, researchers frequently considered bisexual, gay, and lesbian student development in the language of a monolithic construct—that of the "homosexual" (Rhoads, 1997). As our understanding of both similarity and difference have become more refined, the fields of developmental psychology and sociology especially have contributed to our understanding of how young adults, particularly those in college, come to know themselves as nonheterosexual. The research-based developmental frameworks at our disposal, which once posited these identities only in terms of deviance (Mitchell, 1978), now offer empowering and affirming possibilities associated with claiming a BGLT identity.

Contemporary models of queer identity development have approached the issue from the perspective of completion of particular developmental tasks, arrival at particular life stages, or negotiation of one's identity in relation to other salient identities (Ritter and Terndrup, 2002). Each has made different contributions to the knowledge base available about bisexual, gay, lesbian, transgender, and queer students. Each also has limitations, principally stemming from the ideological assumptions at play in the theories themselves; caution must be exercised in adopting any one model as relevant to all. As Bilodeau and Renn (2005) noted, "Practitioners and scholars have an ethical responsibility to understand what the underlying assumptions of the models are, what each [model] purports to describe, on what populations or premises the models were based, and whose interests are served by different models and their uses" (pp. 36–37).

Scholars have similarly cautioned against considering current models of bisexual, gay, and lesbian student development sufficiently attentive to sample size and diversity of study participants, saliency of data collection methods, and complexity (or lack thereof) of theoretical lenses by which participants' perspectives are analyzed and interpreted (Bieschke, Eberz, and Wilson, 2000; Bilodeau and Renn, 2005; Evans and others, 2010). Nevertheless, understanding the foundational theories of bisexual, gay, and lesbian student development—along with their limitations—is essential to conceptualizing their needs as they go about the business of becoming healthy, well-adjusted adults.

Toward the goal of examining these differences, four perspectives of particular historical importance are explored: (1) theories of stage development as advanced by Cass (1984) and Troiden (1979); (2) D'Augelli's framework (1994b) of life span development; (3) Fassinger's theory (1998) of group and individual bisexual, gay, and lesbian identity development; and (4) theories that situate the role of intersectionality in bisexual, gay, and lesbian identity development (Abes, Jones, and McEwen, 2007; Jones and McEwen, 2000). Transgender student development, related to but distinct from models used to describe students' sense of their emerging bisexual, gay, or lesbian sexual orientation, are explored in the next chapter.

Cass's Theory of Homosexual Identity Development

After postulating a theory of homosexual identity development in 1979, Australian psychologist Vivienne Cass shifted her focus to determining the specific contours of "the homosexual experience as experienced and perceived by homosexuals themselves" (Cass, 1984, p. 143). Analyzing survey data gleaned from 178 self-identified gay participants (109 men and 69 women) detailing their journey toward self-acceptance, Cass posited a six-stage model of initiation of and adjustment to a homosexual identity: identity confusion, identity comparison, identity tolerance, identity acceptance, identity pride, and identity synthesis. In this model, individuals begin from a point of initial awakening, experienced as identity confusion, where they have a sense of themselves as sexually different from others. In the second stage, a watershed moment ensues as the individual decides whether a homosexual identity is desirable or not by conducting identity comparison between one's self and others. Those who are able to sustain the notion of themselves as gay can proceed through the next stages; those who cannot may be frozen in this stage of development, feeling a deep sense of disconnect between their innate identities and their desired lives. Contact with others who identify as gay may facilitate self-acceptance.

In the third stage, identity tolerance, the individual seeks out contacts with others but is not yet prepared to embrace the concept of self as homosexual. Typically, this stage requires assumption of a double identity—a public self, shared with heterosexuals, and a private self, shared only with other homosexuals. The weight of straddling the line between one's private and public selves either results in a sense of frozen identity or propels one forward to seek out community that affirms the decision to be more stable, and public, in one's identity as gay.

The social support afforded by immersion into contact with homosexuals facilitates movement into the fourth stage, identity acceptance. In this stage, one alternates between an openly homosexual identity when in the company of others and "passing" or concealing one's homosexual identity when in the presence of those who are not. "Selective disclosure" to those whom the individual feels can be trusted is a common practice at this stage (Cass, 1984, p. 152). Those who have access to a community of other homosexuals are likely to move forward; Cass theorized that without this stage, one cannot easily move into the fifth stage, identity pride. In this stage, one becomes a loyal and enthusiastic member of a tribe, no longer hampered by a sense of deficiency or abnormality. A desire to name (and fight) stigmatization replaces a sense of shame. Interestingly, in a move symbolic of what lay ahead in the evolution of sexual identity development theory, Cass asserted that one's ability to move through the stages depends, to a large degree, on the experiences one has with others.

When moments of confrontation regarding one's homosexual identity are unexpectedly positive, the final stage, identity synthesis, occurs. The homosexual person shifts into viewing his or her sexual identity as one aspect of who he or she is, in concert with other aspects of identity, giving "rise to feelings of peace and stability" (Cass, 1984, p. 153). The person then operates from this place of integration, being known both openly and to one's self as gay and seeing that aspect of his or her life as part of an integrated, positive whole.

Despite the significant contribution it made to our understanding of the ways that individuals discover their homosexual identity, Cass's theory has been critiqued along several lines. Kauffman and Johnson (2004) noted that Cass's theory disregards the significance of how others perceive us and the impact of those perceptions on our own self-image: their research with gay men and lesbians nearly twenty years after the emergence of Cass's theory revealed the crucial extent to which others' positive perceptions shaped participants' ability to continue claiming a gay or lesbian identity. Additionally, Kauffman and Johnson found that romantic relationships with same-sex partners largely influenced the sense of self that individuals developed. As one participant explained, "Being with the first woman affected my identity because we were seen as a couple and confirmed everybody else's knowledge of my identity" (Kauffman and Johnson, 2004, p. 824). This type of experience calls into the question the notion that individuals can develop a sense of a BGLT identity without immersion in relationships and community. Additionally, because Cass's theory was developed from clinical work with adults of many differing ages, the stages or steps of BGLT identity development may not fully apply to traditional-age college students with any specificity.

It would be safe to assume that like most stage theories, Cass's theory implicitly asserts that with each progressive stage, individuals become more confident and well adjusted in their new identities. To test this notion, Halpin and Allen (2004) evaluated the stage at which 425 men ages twelve to sixty-four self-rated on Cass's ladder and the extent to which they felt happy, experienced higher self-esteem, and were satisfied with their lives. Surprisingly, they found that the middle stages—identity tolerance and acceptance—created the most stress for those experiencing them, and thus may require additional support for those going through these stages. The authors hypothesized that although one may be coming to terms with his or her identity, the process of coming out to others and risking (or managing) stigma, judgment, and rejection may cause significant anxiety. The road to full acceptance to a gay identity thus may be rockier than Cass portended.

Troiden's Theory of Homosexual Identity Development

The limitations of language of necessity can shape our understanding of how individuals come out as bisexual, gay, lesbian, and transgender. Though admittedly limited by the language of "stage" or "step," sociologist Richard Troiden (1979, 1994) advanced a theory of homosexual identity development that he likened more to a spiral than to a stepwise process. Troiden was not comfortable associating homosexual experiences with homosexual identity per se; he argued that many people have same-sex romantic experiences but never identify, or present themselves, as homosexual. For that reason, his stages imply a gradual realization, then publicly avowed narrative, of being gay that solidifies those who are gay from those who act gay.

Because he was writing from the vantage point of a sociologist, Troiden leaned more heavily toward considering the distinctive social contexts in which those who identify as homosexual emerge. In the first stage, sensitization, gay men and lesbians identify prepubescent experiences that, although they may not point directly to admission of a gay identity, hint at the relevance of homosexuality to their lives in the future. These experiences include a sense of marginality, of not fitting in socially with other peers because of differing personae or favored activities; these activities were rarely sexual in nature but centered more around a generalized feeling of being different. A lack of interest in other-sex peers, as opposed to a confirmed interest in same-sex peers, defined this sense of difference. Any sexual experimentation occurring during this time was not experienced as a signpost for being gay as such but rather as a confirmation of difference that would gain meaning later when the individual had a social or sexual context of norms and practices in which to understand this behavior.

In the second stage, identity confusion, the individual (usually in adolescence) begins to experience a profound sense of disconnect with others and begins to wonder whether he or she is actually homosexual. One begins to grapple with the stigma of being homosexual expressed by others while also experiencing homosexual feelings (sometimes coupled with lack of heterosexual feelings) and having few or no social outlets to safely explore and discuss these feelings. The individual proceeds to work through this confusion in one of five ways: (1) denial of the experiences and feelings; (2) attempts to repair one's self toward more normative desires, often involving professional help; (3) avoidance of interactions, acquisition of additional knowledge, or reflection on feelings that will confirm the homosexual identity; (4) redefinition of one's self as having a one-time feeling for same-sex attraction, as being bisexual, or attributing the attraction to being drunk or another mediating factor; or (5) acceptance of both one's desires and one's identity as a homosexual (Troiden, 1994).

In the third stage, identity assumption, the individual has now come to terms with a self-identity as homosexual and begins to present a public identity as such. It is what is known as "coming out," and it is typified by development of tolerance for one's identity, socialization experiences with other homosexuals, sexual experimentation, and becoming part of various queer communities and subcultures. Troiden notes that studies suggest that gay men and lesbians appear to arrive at this stage at different ages, with women (between the ages of twenty-one and twenty-three) claiming a lesbian identity slightly later than men (between the ages of nineteen and twenty-one), and that women tend to do so as a result of intense romantic relationships with women, whereas men do so as a result of more casual and short-term interactions with other gay men (such as in bars and other social settings). Writing in the mid-1990s, Troiden acknowledged that these conclusions are likely outdated and that men specifically were probably more likely to discover a gay male identity through romantic relationships as a result of fear of casual intimacy associated with the AIDS epidemic (Troiden, 1994).

During this time, those who are able to initiate and make contact with a gay community appear to make progress toward a sense of belonging to a greater whole. According to Troiden (1994), "Personally meaningful contacts with experienced homosexuals also [enable] neophytes to see that homosexuality is socially organized, and that a group exists to which they may belong, which diminishes feelings of solitude and alienation" (p. 206). Also during this time, Troiden observed that many make a commitment to "passing"—identifying as homosexual internally without declaring an identity to heterosexual family, friends, and others. The energy required of those who pass serves to distract from pursuit of a healthy and integrated sense of self and can also result in lower self-esteem.

Troiden's fourth and final stage, commitment, is accompanied by the sense that the individual has taken on an identity for his or her lifetime and is settling in to that reality rather than pursuing transformation or hiding. By both embracing the identity within themselves and presenting the identity to the outside world, they may adopt a range of "stigma-management strategies" (p. 208) that will enable them to thrive in a different way. They become observably more content and more likely to declare their identity to others, including family members, friends, and other acquaintances. They may shift from simply passing to blending, whereby they may avoid regularly declaring to others and reserving the identity for their close social circle. Others embody a sense of personal pride about their gay identity, no longer distancing themselves from it but seeing it as a valued and valuable aspect of their identities. All four stages, according to Troiden, may be embraced, deferred, or avoided based on a personal social setting, relationships, community connections, and access to support and other resources. The model thus suggests a progressive multifaceted manner of embracing one's identity through the selective adoption of strategies to explore and affirm one's self as gay or lesbian and to look to others in the community for a sense of solidarity, pride, and belonging. Like Cass's model, Troiden's model has been criticized for lack of attention to the developmentally different experiences (Diamond, 2005; Savin-Williams and Diamond, 2001) among bisexual, gay, and lesbian people of different races and cultures (Eliason, 1996) and because these studies typically do not document the real-time experiences of the age cohort (adolescent youth) most likely to experience the stress of coming out (Savin-Williams, 2001).

D'Augelli's Life Span Model

Referring to the concept that a more complex set of circumstances, personal qualities, and social or cultural factors are at work in the development of a bisexual, gay, or lesbian identity, D'Augelli (1994b) noted, life span models "involve the explication of patterns of dynamic interaction of multiple factors over time in the development of an individual person. The developing man or woman must be understood in context" (pp. 121–122). Examining one's culture, history, family and other significant personal relationships and taking into account the fact that people change throughout the course of their lives provide a fuller picture of how one comes to understand same-sex attraction as related to, but not synonymous with, one's composite identity. D'Augelli employed the concept of plasticity—the idea that human functioning is subject to changes in context and conditions over time—to explain individuals' myriad reactions to experiences with same-sex desire and actions. Far from having no agency over these dynamic processes, individuals, too, shape and make meaning of their queer identities "out of necessity, due to a heterosexist culture that provides no routine socialization for lesbian and gay development" (1994b, p. 127).

D'Augelli's life span model thus incorporates context, dynamism, and agency, suggesting that individuals' identities may shift or may remain relatively fixed depending on individual life history; the regularities of certain kinds of experiences that he noted in his studies of lesbians and gay men suggest broad themes rather than fixed stages. The first of six interactive processes that DAugelli (1994a) identified is known as "exiting a heterosexual identity" and is typified by realization that one is having feelings of same-sex attraction and that one is willing to both name it and tell others about it. A college student may visit a meeting of the campus student support group for queer students as part of this process (Evans and others, 2010). A second process is known as "developing a personal lesbian, gay, or bisexual identity status," which includes examining the various models of queer identity available in one's immediate cultural or historical context, choosing one or more versions of these identities to adhere to. According to D'Augelli, this process is typically done in community with other BGL people and in settings where the meaning of being BGL may be constantly redefined and negotiated. "Developing a BGL social identity" happens as individuals develop a social network of both BGL people and supportive, in-the-know allies through the process of disclosure and adaptation to relationships that are inevitably transformed by disclosure. This process is typically referred to as "coming out," and for most BGL people, it is a lifelong process of revelation, especially to those in one's life who are heterosexual.

Because family relationships are viewed as central to the formation of one's sense of self as bisexual, gay, or lesbian, the process of "claiming an identity as a bisexual, gay, or lesbian offspring" is given its own separate considerations in D'Augelli's process; the redefinition of parental and sibling relationships after one comes out is significant and can be improved with time and education. "Developing a bisexual, gay, or lesbian intimacy status," becoming romantically and sexually involved with others of the same gender, is complicated by the fact that there are few if any relatable role models in society at large (though this situation has markedly improved in the last twenty years). This process may be of most salience to college students, who are establishing independence from parents and are now free to pursue romantic relationships outside the watchful eye of parents.

The importance of developing social, communal, and even political bonds is typified by the process of "entering a bisexual, gay, or lesbian community" and can be marked by personal risk (as one comes out in a society where legal protections for BGL people continue to be limited). Some bisexual, gay, or lesbian individuals never pursue a life of full and complete "outness" based on their perceptions of the risks they may sustain; college students attending religiously conservative colleges may conceal their identity from others as one example of the cost-calculation this process entails.

Understanding students' experiences with these processes can be helpful in creating college and university environments that support their growth.

Research conducted on the salience of D'Augelli's model for understanding bisexual, gay, and lesbian college student experiences suggests that numerous factors, including peer support and acceptance, residence hall climate, easy identification of faculty and staff role models, and transparent policies for confronting harassment of BGL students, all played a role in facilitating the processes of development so crucial for the emergence of a positive, self-defined BGL identity (Evans, 2001; Evans and Broido, 1999; Sanlo, 1998).

Fassinger's Model of Bisexual, Gay, and Lesbian Identity Development in Context

As noted by D'Augelli (1994a), individuals coming to a sense of their own bisexual, gay, or lesbian identity rarely do so in a vacuum: the places, relationships, and traditions that shape their life experiences are a powerful backdrop for the way that their process unfolds and must be considered part and parcel of coming to know one's self, whether one conceives of that transition in stages, in a spiral, or in a more process-oriented fashion. As discussed in the previous chapter, the group membership aspect of coming out as bisexual, gay, or lesbian is especially salient among college students; since Stonewall, BGL students have mobilized and created community in an effort to minimize isolation and as an integral part of the new world they endeavored to create on campus. The synthesis of the individual's coming to know of one's self as BGL and coming to know one's self in community with others is deeply reflected by the work of Ruth Fassinger (Evans and others, 2010).

Fassinger (1998), deriving her thinking from participant perspectives that were more racially and ethnically diverse and including more women than in previous studies, developed a stage-based model of identity development that considers how other group memberships dovetail, intersect with, and sometimes confound an individual's sense of his or her BGL identity. Each aspect of one's progression has two branches, one for self and one for self in relation to a larger BGLT reference group or community. In the first stage, much like Cass's exiting a heterosexual identity or Troiden's sensitization, is a sense of "awareness," wherein the individual begins to grapple with a sense of difference from one's peers. In the next stage, "exploration," the individual begins to explore his or her same-sex attractions and desires while also making efforts to become (or imagine themselves becoming) part of a group of people with the same identity. As one begins to create an individualized sense of self that is bisexual, gay, or lesbian and to simultaneously confirm one's group affiliations and loyalties, one is said to be in the third stage—"deepening commitment."

The final stage, "internalization and synthesis," is defined for individuals as integrating one's same-sex or bisexual sexual orientation into his or her larger identity and embracing and communicating minority group membership across different social and relational contexts. According to Fassinger (1998), "The branches of the model are assumed to be mutually catalytic, in that addressing the developmental tasks in either branch is likely to produce some movement in the other branch" (p. 18). The mutually reinforcing effects of the individual's or group's relationship helps to empower students as they move through and within the stages, gaining strength from solidarity that then serves as scaffolding for them to make increasingly public commitments regarding their own identity.

Beyond the Monolithic Queer: Developmental Theory in Twenty-First-Century Context

Although Cass's, Troiden's, D'Augelli's, and Fassinger's models for conceptualizing bisexual, gay, and lesbian college student development have been enormously influential in shaping educational practice and environments, a major critique of these findings is that the research to date does not reflect the complexity of identity that typifies today's college students. Theories of BGLT student development put forth in the first twenty years after Stonewall may offer a tempting but oversimplified view of how individuals arrive at sexual and gender identity. And although these models provide useful signposts toward viewing students in process, it is important to reconcile these urges to simplify with the actual complexity of student identity. Rhoads (1997) asserted that resisting the pull of framing BGL student development in a monolithic way and assuming one generic queer subject is critical to truly knowing these students as individuals.

To illustrate this point, Rhoads (1994, 1997) shared the intersection and disconnect noted in one study of forty individual gay and bisexual male students at an eastern U.S. college. In analyzing their coming-out narratives, he found several commonalities among the men in his study, including the importance of hanging out in communal settings (such as bars and coffee shops) to solidify one's identity, adopting a particular style (camp) to demarcate one's identity in contrast to heterosexual men, and using a different nature of conversation and other interactions with gay men as opposed to the nature of interacting with straight friends. Points of tension, where the sample had little or no uniformity, arose when participants discussed their relative and divergent types of interest in gay politics and visibility, the uniquely "raced" experience of gay men of color versus the white men in the study, and the marginalization of men who identified as bisexual. These tensions point to the fact that developmental theories that posit "sameness" of experience between and among students may be misleading in their generality. Using developmental theory to make sense of individual student's behaviors without using theories to predict particular phases in a BGLTQ student's life is thus the appropriate way to proceed.

Other studies of gay men reflecting on their college years (Dilley, 2002a, 2010) revealed that historicity appears to heavily influence, if not drive, the process these men experienced in coming to terms with their identity. Their narratives demonstrated that they were part of a typology that included seven distinct categories of expression: homosexual, closeted, gay, queer, "normal," parallel, and denying. As historical changes transpired, alumni across five decades of participation in higher education viewed themselves and their sexuality differently and incorporated these differences into their process of making meaning of who they are. This framework suggests nuances that escape understanding when we examine student experiences in only one moment; Dilley asserts that the drawback of doing so is the mistaken assumption that "all men in college who do not identify as heterosexual have a fairly homogeneous, unified pattern of experiences and understandings" (2002a, p. 7). After examining the narratives of students in the last decade, Dilley (2010) added two additional categories—"twitter twinks" and "lads without labels"—to the ever-expanding typology of gay male identities.

Other researchers have indicated that looking at the context-laden experiences of particular subsets of BGL students—for example, African American gay and bisexual men (Patton, 2011; Washington and Wall, 2006), lesbian women (Abes and Jones, 2004; Diamond, 2000), bisexual students (O'Brien, 1998; Robin and Hamner, 2000), and queer students with disabilities (Harley, Nowak, Gassaway, and Savage, 2002; Henry, Fuerth, and Figliozzi, 2010)—reveals nuances of developmental theories that have yet to be sufficiently addressed. Like all research, the body of literature about the identities of BGL students is framed in particular ways, with particular inherent values in the way questions are constructed, the manner in which data are collected, and the way these data are analyzed. Looking beyond the presumed frames of research conducted in the early years after Stonewall helps to bring depth and multidimensionality to queer students' experiences.

Students of Color and Bisexual, Gay, and Lesbian Identity Development

As research has demonstrated, students of color navigating the coming-out process must contend with the double bind of racism and homophobia in the educational environment (Diaz and Kosciw, 2009; Dube and Savin-Williams, 1999; Evans and Wall, 1991; Wall and Evans, 2000). Environmental and institutional stressors, lack of role models among BGLT faculty and staff, and pressures to represent one's race in the frameworks of the dominant culture can make the process of embracing an additional nonmajority identity complicated, to say the least. For men of color in college, this reality is compounded by pressures to perform a masculinity that is authentic while it positions these men's success solely in relation to accepted, dominant cultural norms of manhood (Harper, 2004; Harris, 2008; Stevens, 2004). African Americans who claim a BGL sexual identity often experience the double bind of racism and homophobia in sharp relief. As noted by black gay activist and author Boykin (1996), "For black lesbians and gays, unlike straight blacks, our sexual orientation does not insulate us from the oppression of homophobia, and unlike white lesbians and gays, our skin color does not insulate us from the oppression of racism. We can cocoon ourselves in isolated artificial environments, but the moment we step out of our protective spaces, we are targets again, prey of the dominant culture" (p. 99).

Studies of black men navigating a gay or bisexual identity development process suggest that men in this group may experience strong pressure to conform to highly traditional standards of masculinity, to conceal their sexuality to some or all of their community (often referred to as being on the "down low"), and to work hard to maintain connections with heterosexual men as a way of establishing power in their communities (Boykin, 1996; Christian, 2005; Icard, 1996; Loiacano, 1989). The cost of this double oppression is high, as experiences with both racism and homophobia are highly correlated with depression in African American bisexual and gay men (Alexander, 2004). College can be a time when these challenges are accentuated: studies of gay and bisexual men of color in college show that as they develop along an axis of sexual orientation, they may also experience disconnects between their sense of self as a queer man and a black man, pressure to conform to their own (and the culture at large's) restrictive definition of masculinity, complexity regarding their relationships to other men and to women, and conflict with their spirituality (Dumas, 1998; Washington and Wall, 2006).

In understanding the experiences of black gay and bisexual men, institutional context appears to matter a great deal. Studying black gay men at predominantly white institutions, Harris (2003) found that black gay men feel pulled between the small but visible community of other black students on campus and a small (and largely invisible) gay student minority. Conversely, one study of black gay and bisexual men studying at an HBCU noted that moving in this environment has its own set of complicating factors and that although men in these institutions experience less overt racism, they may experience significant challenges determining authenticity, experiencing and acting on both same-sex and other-sex desire, and carefully choosing when one is out and one is not because of the consequences entailed. Peer support appears to be the most vital factor in establishing a sense of safety as a queer man in this environment (Patton, 2011).

African American men thus experience a complicated process of coming to terms with their gay or bisexual identity that is compounded by negotiating a sense of their own masculinity in the campus culture and the culture of home. They may experience rejection from their home and communities for being gay and thus not masculine. They may experience rejection in the gay community for being perceived outside the ideal gay male stereotype, and they may be "exoticized" by white gay male peers. Each of these experiences can create a sense of isolation or fragmentation as they work to integrate these differing aspects of who they are.

Inarguably, these aspects of black gay and bisexual men's identity development make the process of coming out more complex, and evidence suggests that other subgroups of queer people of color—Latino men, black, Asian, and Latina lesbian and bisexual women, and Native American (also known as "Two Spirit") gay, bisexual, and transgender individuals—experience similar challenges as they negotiate the racism of the dominant culture and the homo- and biphobia of both the dominant culture and their culture of origin (Cintron, 2000; Estrada and Rutter, 2006; Ferguson and Howard-Hamilton, 2000; Fukuyama and Ferguson, 2000; Wilson, 1996). To more accurately understand the multiple dimensions of identity development, researchers have posited a model of bisexual, gay, and lesbian identity development that more appropriately accounts for the experiences faced by those who bring multiple (and equally salient) strands of identity to the development process.

Intersectionality and Identity Development

Although traditional theories of BGLT identity development add important perspective, intersectionality offers a different, richer lens by which to understand and appreciate students in their BGL identity development. The theory, developed primarily by feminist theorists of color over the last two decades (Collins, 2000; Crenshaw, 1991), seeks to address the lack of representation of diverse subjects in theorizing about social relationships and considers identity in concert with power relations in society (Torres, Jones, and Renn, 2009). Researchers who advance an understanding of student development through the lens of intersectionality posit that individual identities are complex and made up of our complete social personae—our gender identity, race, social class, family history, ability status, and many other individual traits. These traits and the ways we come to understand and legitimize some over others is a process of social construction, one in which we are an active participant but are acted upon by social, cultural, and historical forces beyond our control

(Weber, 1998). Intersectionality offers a deeper understanding of who we are and how we become the person we are through this constructive process, including how we develop a relationship to our sexual orientation and gender identity. Thinking about queer identity development in intersectional ways has a distinct advantage over traditional ways of imagining ourselves. As Clark (2005) asserts, "Unlike exclusively centric analysis in which one social identity dimension is examined, almost as if in a vacuum, and then *juxtaposed*, in a highly dichotomous fashion, with other dimensions, intersectional analysis enables race and gender and socioeconomic class, etc., to be woven together in complex, competing and synergistic, complementary and cacophonous, ultimately tapestrial manners toward the chrysalis of more exacting sociopolitical realities" (p. 46).

How do BGLT people grappling with multiple identities cope as the pressures bear down on them to negotiate their race, ethnicity, culture, and other aspects of who they are with being bisexual, gay, or lesbian? Pope and Reynolds's (1991) conceptualization suggested that they might identify in one of four ways. They may choose to align with one group to the exclusion of others, based on external pressure from family, friends, or culture, doing so passively or in a way that demonstrates more agency and is self-chosen. Individuals may, alternatively, identify with different identity groups at different times, depending on the circumstances and the personal and social costs associated with doing so, in a disconnected fashion. Finally, some may find it preferable to honor their multiple identities at once, seeking or creating a new identity group with which to affiliate. These individuals at the nexus of multiple identities also strategize effectively toward achieving a holistic identity and manage to integrate these multiple identities into a unified sense of self (Pope and Reynolds, 1991). Without judging or advancing any one of these four possible responses to multiple oppressions as the only or best way, Pope and Reynolds nonetheless assert that helping professionals "must also be able to understand and facilitate this integration of identity" (p. 179).

Building on the work of Pope and Reynolds (1991), one model that conceptualizes the specific ways that college students negotiate identity with other aspects of self was advanced by Jones and McEwen (2000). Interviewing ten undergraduate women with multiple identities along axes of race, ethnicity, religion, sexual orientation, and social class, the researchers found that ten aspects of the identity development process are relatively consistent across the group: (1) relative salience of identity dimensions in relation to difference; (2) multiple ways in which race matters; (3) multiple layers of identity; (4) braiding of gender with other dimensions; (5) importance of cultural identifications and cultural values; (6) influence of family and background experiences; (7) current experiences and situational factors; (8) relational, inclusive values and guiding personal beliefs; (9) career decisions and future planning; and (10) search for identity. Although each dimension of individuals' identity and the aspects that shape it must be understood in reference to all others, participants consistently named the existence of a "core self," an "inner identity," that they protect from view but is essential to their sense of who they are in the world (Jones and McEwen, 2000, p. 408). They discussed how they go about engaging in self-definition, balancing the external and internal pressures associated with their multiple identities in a process fashion that is highly dependent on context and less amenable to a stage or step model of becoming.

With additional data gleaned from further research with lesbian college women of diverse races and ethnicities, Abes, Jones, and McEwen (2007) proposed a comprehensive way to understand the manner in which participants make meaning of their multiple identities in context (see Figure 1). These participants revealed that the process by which they understand the intersection of their sexuality with other identity dimensions is typified in one of three ways—formulaic, transitional, or foundational—reflecting a construct previously articulated in research by Baxter Magolda (2001). Exhibiting formulaic meaning making, one participant's assessment of her identity was heavily bound up with contextual influences, including what she was taught and told about her identities. These preformed conceptions of identity are taken as absolutes, and individuals in formulaic meaning making define themselves based on them accordingly, without extending personal analysis to the accuracy or inaccuracy of proscriptions or truths. Students operating from this framework tend to reject connections between and among their identities and are less interested in critiquing messages they have received for salience to their own life-avoiding complexity.

FIGURE 1

Reconceptualized Model of Multiple Dimensions of Identity

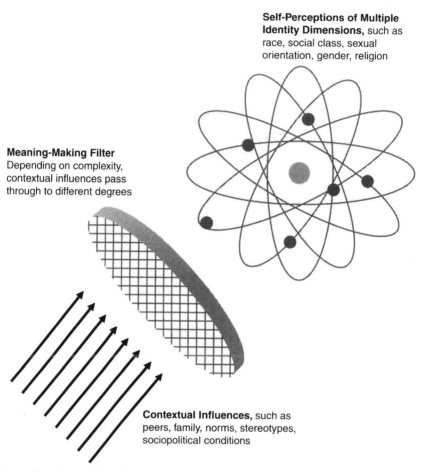

Self-Perceptions of Multiple Identity Dimensions, such as race, social class, sexual orientation, gender, religion

Meaning-Making Filter
Depending on complexity, contextual influences pass through to different degrees

Contextual Influences, such as peers, family, norms, stereotypes, sociopolitical conditions

Source: Abes, Jones, and McEwen, 2007, p. 7.

Transitional meaning making is characterized by a critical departure from formulaic thinking, as students begin to grapple with the inherent contradictions in and among the teaching they have received or observed about their identities. They may experience dissonance as they struggle to reconcile multiple aspects of their identities such as when their sexuality comes in conflict with their race or ethnicity, and contextual influences such as family and friends seek to delimit their conception of what is possible for their own lives. Students in transitional meaning making are beginning to use the filter of judgment, based on experience and a strengthened sense of their own ability to discern what is best for their lives, to parse out truth from belief.

Finally, students negotiating a lesbian identity with other aspects of their lives who can comfortably resist stereotypes and messaging to arrive at a more authentic and self-derived persona are said to be practicing foundational meaning making. In this frame of mind, a student may use life experience, especially that with oppression, to solidify the importance of creating an individually authentic self and may engage with political and social change as a necessary outgrowth of these experiences. Multiple aspects of identity may be thought of as acting in parallel but are not necessarily integrated in any particular sense.

Action to advance one's sense of belonging and safety in the world from a place of genuine agency as opposed to coercion or belief is the mainstay of the ways that students in this kind of thinking make sense of their multiple intersecting (but not necessarily interwoven) identities.

Regarding the core identity identified by Jones and McEwen (2000), students in the follow-up study described it as less static and more malleable than previously imagined by participants in the first study. Considering their sexual orientation in relation to other identities, participants in Abes, McEwen, and Jones's study (2007) described the core "and some of their social identities as interacting dynamically. For instance, socially constructed identities might move in and out of the core depending on contextual influences and the changing meaning individuals make of these identities" (p. 15).

The truism that each student experiences the intersection of his or her various identities and sexual orientation differently should not be taken as indication that students must navigate these processes alone or without support. Student affairs administrators and faculty with responsibility for shaping optimal environments to support students in the multiplicity of their identities can do so by honoring the language students use to describe themselves, engaging all students, including (and especially) majority-identity students, in conversations about identity, working with those representing cultural and ethnic life on campus to foment discussions about BGLT identity, and featuring face time with visible role models who are successfully negotiating multiple identities in their own lives (Jones and McEwen, 2000; Poynter and Washington, 2005; Schueler, Hoffman, and Peterson, 2009). Researchers also point to a strong need to continue to explore, refine, and make complex the previous (and possibly misleading) neatness of previous theories drawn from diverse student samples (Abes, Jones, and McEwen, 2007). They implore educators to think beyond single-dimension models of identity development to consider students' identities as mosaic, the interlocking tiles working to create a sense of self in dynamic negotiation with students' multiple cultures and contexts.

Impediments to BGL Student Development in College

Models of BGL student development offer useful scaffolding upon which to construct supportive campus environments. It is important also to recognize—and address—the factors that impede healthy development of BGL students. The stress of coping with being marginalized manifests itself in a variety of ways; recent research suggests that BGL-identified students are more likely to abuse alcohol and other illicit drugs in college in direct relation to questioning or struggling with a BGL identity as well as experiencing the effects of a chilly campus climate (Reed, Prado, Matsumoto, and Amaro, 2010; Tailey, Sher, and Littlefield, 2010). It would be too simplistic, however, to assume that availability of resources equals better adjustment and in turn more healthy behaviors. Instead, in one large-scale national study, the availability of resources for BGLT student life on campus was positively associated with queer women's smoking and queer men's binge drinking (Eisenberg and Wechsler, 2003).

Disaggregating the BGL student community yields important information about specific barriers to development. Gay men in college, for example, appear to be at risk for specific negative health outcomes. Despite nearly three decades of safer-sex messaging encouraging condom use, gay men in college with multiple partners are experiencing "safe sex fatigue" and reporting lower rates of regular condom use (Kellogg, 2002). Gay men in college are also more likely than their nongay male peers to contract HIV and viral hepatitis, to develop adverse health effects from tobacco use, and to exhibit dependency on alcohol (Rhodes, McCoy, Wilkin, and Wolfson, 2009).

Queer women students appear to struggle with their own impediments to healthy development in college. One study (Bostwick and others, 2007) found that bisexual women in college, although drinking less (in terms of quantity) than their straight-identified female counterparts, were just as likely to report drinking-related problems such as being embarrassed or disturbed by something they did, performing poorly academically, and contemplating suicide. Those advocating for improved health services for bisexuals in college and university health services note that bisexual people experience greater frequency of anxiety, depression, suicidality, and self-injurious behavior than other sexual identity groups (Oswalt, 2009). The pressures of dealing with a homo- and biphobic culture may manifest in other ways for queer women as well. While the social factors that press women to conform to body image differ, both lesbians and heterosexual women appear to experience similar levels of disordered eating and body image problems while also being likely to express self-judgment for participating in these behaviors (Beren, Hayden, Wilfley, and Striegel-Moore, 1997; Striegel-Moore, Tucker, and Hsu, 1990).

These negative health outcomes and what they portend for BGLT student development require new and creative thinking about interventions that speak to the daily challenges faced by BGLT students on campus, coupled with research to support best practices that prevent BGLT students from turning societal discrimination inward to cope in unhealthy ways.

Conclusion

Forty years ago when Stonewall happened, the student affairs profession was just beginning to understand the ways that young adults develop with respect to a bisexual, gay, or lesbian sexual orientation and just beginning to see how these processes take shape in college students' lives. As students come to know themselves as individuals, as members of communities, and as learners, it is more important than ever to enable them to know who they are in the world. The increasing emphasis on extending beyond one's familiar zone to embrace and explore the realities of a global economy is a mandate of the twenty-first century educational experience. Students' knowledge of self in relation to others and in context is essential to being able to communicate across differences (Nieto, 1996; Pope, Reynolds, and Mueller, 2004).

We now know that facilitating students' development means more than seeing them as one-dimensional beings, along any axis of identity. With time and careful consideration of how we come to be who we are, we have developed a more nuanced and complex understanding of what it means to know one's self as bisexual, gay, or lesbian. We need to acknowledge the fact that sexual orientation and gender identity, like race, social class, ability, and religious identity, are among the most formative aspects of one's life experience. Providing students with the tools to know themselves and in turn to know others enriches their college experience and prepares them more fruitfully for democratic citizenship in the twenty-first century.

Transgender Student Issues and Development After Stonewall

> On more than one occasion, I asked, 'but what about transgender?
>
> —Fried, 2000, p. 255

TRANSGENDER COLLEGE STUDENTS are a diverse group, comprising many different individuals and groups who transgress gender norms. Typically, their lived experience of their gender is different from the gender corresponding to their assigned sex at birth (Feinberg, 1996).

Who Are Transgender College Students?

Transgender individuals identify in numerous ways—simply as transgender (or trans) or with another identity such as transsexual (male-to-female, or female-to-male), cross-dresser, genderqueer, gender-variant, and other identities. Exhibit 1 describes some of the varieties of transgender identity and some terminology associated with each identity. It is important to note that transgender identities vary widely and that not everyone who identifies as transgender fits neatly into one specific category or label (Human Rights Campaign, n.d.). Additionally, transgender is both an umbrella term, signifying the entire community, and a specific identifier for a subset of trans individuals.

Although their contributions to BGLT campus activism, especially in the years during and after Stonewall, have been overlooked or marginalized, transgender individuals attending American colleges and universities are growing in visibility and voice (Brune, 2007; Quart, 2008; Schnetzler and Conant,

EXHIBIT 1

Transgender Identities

Identity	Definition
Transgender	A broad range of people who experience or express their gender differently from what most people expect, either in terms of expressing a gender that does not match the sex listed on their original birth certificate or physically changing their sex. It is an umbrella term that includes people who are transsexual, cross-dressers, or otherwise gender noncomforming.
Transsexual	A person who has changed, or is in the process of changing, his or her physical sex to conform to his or her internal sense of gender identity. The term can also be used to describe people who, without undergoing medical treatment, identify and live their lives full-time as a member of a gender different from their birth sex. Transsexuals may refer to themselves as "MTF" (for male-to-female, indicating the direction of their transition) or "FTM."
Gender nonconforming/ Genderqueer	People who are not transsexuals or cross-dressers but who still express a nonstandard gender identity or do not conform to traditional gender norms. Some gender-nonconforming women act "butch" or in a stereotypically masculine manner, and some men act "femme" or in a stereotypically feminine manner, but these indiviuals do not identify as the opposite gender and do not present themselves as such full time.
Cross-dresser	People who wear the clothing or accoutrements (such as makeup and accessories) considered by society to correspond to the "opposite sex." Cross-dressers can be either male to female or female to male. Unlike transsexuals, they typically do not seek to change their physical characteristics permanently or desire to live full time as the opposite gender. Cross-dressers are sometimes called *transvestites,* but that term is considered pejorative today.

Source: Adapted from Human Rights Campaign, n.d.

2009; Tilsley, 2010). Transgender students, faculty, and staff are not only taking their rightful place on campus but are also infusing college environments with activism centered around recognition of and respect for their (and all) gender identities. Colleges and universities are in turn being transformed by their presence toward greater inclusion and support for expression of all gender identities.

Although it is important to consider transgender students as a subset of the population of students who identify as BGLT, it is equally critical not to presume that being transgender is the same thing as being bisexual, gay, or lesbian or even that a necessarily dependent relationship exists between those who identify as being BGL and those who are T (Califia, 1997). In fact, sexual orientation and gender identity are separate and distinct concepts and should not be conflated: because transgender people express their gender in myriad ways, they also experience their sexuality in myriad ways, including as straight, bisexual, gay, lesbian, and forms of sexual identity that defy all of these categorizations. Although much of what has been written about the needs of transgender college students has presumed them to be synonymous with those who identify as bisexual, gay, or lesbian, their concerns are distinctive. Researchers have argued for more careful attention to these differences to better serve trans students (Beemyn, 2003a; Dilley, 2004). Transgender people's concerns are connected with those who are bisexual, gay, or lesbian because these identities share a common facet of oppression: by failing to conform to prescribed gender stereotypes for men's and women's behaviors in society, each is "transgressing gender" in different ways. The effects of homophobia are well known; we are just beginning to know the short- and long-term personal and social costs of transphobia, defined as "societal discrimination and stigma of individuals who do not conform to traditional norms of sex and gender" (Sugano, Nemoto, and Operario, 2006, p. 217). As one author noted, "The LGB movement and the transgender movement, although not the same, have too much in common to ignore" (Carter, 2000, p. 274).

In his study of transgender students' experiences as reported in Internet relay chat rooms, Pusch (2003) observed that "transgender students are assumed to have the same issues as gay, lesbian, and bisexual students, which leaves their needs and issues not fully addressed, or even completely understood" (p. 17). What is well understood is the fact that this assumption can have the unintended effect of requiring masking or hiding of transgender individuals as they attempt to blend in with other queer people rather than express their authentic identities (Morgan and Stevens, 2008).

One effect of the masking or hiding required by societal transphobia is the reality that the actual number of transgender individuals living in the United States—and attending American colleges and universities—is not known. Recent surveys estimate the prevalence of some variety of one form of transgender identity, transsexualism, as being somewhere between one in two hundred fifty and one in five hundred individuals (Conway, 2002). Although a recent national survey indicated that nearly 70 percent of transgender individuals are aware of their gender identity between the ages of eighteen and twenty-two (Beemyn, 2007), the gender transition process typically happens following adolescence, and thus it is safe to assume that many who identify as transgender do not come out as such until well after their college years. Rising numbers of students identifying as transgender on both institutional and national surveys (for example, the data reports from the 2009 and 2010 National College Health Assessment surveys, where the reference group of transgender students doubled from 0.1 percent to 0.2 percent in one year) and survey makers' recent attention to inclusion of transgender identity (John Pryor, personal communication, 2011) indicate that claiming a transgender identity is more prevalent among American college students than previously thought.

Transgender Students at Women's Colleges

Thanks to their increased visibility, transgender students' inclusion and belonging have been enhanced at many institutions. Yet at one type of institution—the American women's college—their presence is still contested. In the last decade, women's colleges have seen increasing enrollment of male-identified transgender and genderqueer students, and the presence of these students has sparked controversy and protracted discussions about whether these institutions are transgender students' rightful place (Brune, 2007; Greenaway, 2001;

Morais and Schreiber, 2007; Offman, 2005; Quart, 2008; Raftery, 2003). The presence of transgender students has raised questions about the definition of "woman," whether the word should be defined biologically in terms of students' felt and expressed sense of gender identity, or both. It also raises questions about the admission of students who are born and live their whole lives as men and whether women's colleges can continue to restrict admission to one sex, given that it is clear that students' sex and gender can, and does, change during college.

In the 2006 Sundance video documentary *Transgeneration,* Lucas Cheadle, a trans male student at Smith College, brought his unique experience into the public light and demonstrated that his evolving gender identity has complex implications for his enrollment at this women's college (Smothers, 2006). While struggling with his gender identity, Lucas also felt a deep sense of investment in the college community and in his circle of personal support among students and faculty there. Although the question of his belonging is not easily discerned, research suggests that some student affairs administrators at women's colleges see themselves as supporters and advocates for this community and do not see these roles as being in conflict with their professional responsibilities (Marine, 2009). Student affairs administrators making efforts to understand and support them demonstrated that transgender students are often expected to confine their gender identity to the institution's expectations, even while they are taking steps toward authenticity in their gender expression. Ironically, the sense of personal empowerment Lucas gained as a benefit of attending a women's college may have enabled him to move toward his true identity sooner. Lucas's lived experience thus demonstrates that no easy answers exist to the question of whether single-sex institutions can and will be a safe haven for transgender students in the future.

Transgender Student Development

Because they were developed at a time when researchers' understanding of gender transition was not adequate, traditional student development theories (and the campus policies and practices emanating from them) may be less relevant for students whose gender identity does not conform to their biologically assigned sex or whose gender is in a state of transition. By virtue of their efforts to solidify and assert an internalized sense of gender identity that does not match the gender identity they were assigned at birth, transgender individuals are tasked with negotiating the process of college differently. They must approach all the typical developmental tasks (Chickering and Reisser, 1993) such as determining a purpose and calling, defining themselves academically and vocationally, and developing meaningful interpersonal relationships while they are also establishing who they are and how they choose to both present and be perceived in terms of their gender identity.

At present, the literature on transgender college students is relatively sparse and, as noted previously, is largely subsumed under the general category of LGBT student identity and concerns. To date, three qualitative studies (Bilodeau, 2005a; McKinney, 2005; Pusch, 2005) of the specific experiences of transgender students in college have been published, and they are limited in the extent to which they can be generalized to the population as a whole. The future looks brighter in terms of rounding out the literature; recent dissertations on the topic have explored black transgender students' experiences (Bradley, 2007), student affairs administrators' perceptions of transgender students (Marine, 2009), transgender students' experiences at a rural New England college (Lynch, 2010), and transgender students' experiences with transition in an online community (Pusch, 2003). Published personal narratives of transgender college students shed additional light on the unique challenges associated with transitioning one's gender during this phase even as they represent an admittedly narrow "*n* of one" (Fried, 2000; Rogers, 2000).

Although the full picture of how and in what ways transgender students come to know themselves is still emerging, several theories of identity development help to explain the path taken to a reclaimed sense of gender identity for this population. Devor's fourteen-stage theory (2004), which reflects twenty years of clinical work with the trans community and is informed by theories developed to understand BGL identity development (noted in the previous chapter), sheds light on the gradual, deliberate process toward symbiosis of one's felt sense of gender and one's expressed gender identity. According to Devor, this process begins with a sense of abiding anxiety with one's gender identity, moving next to coping with the dissonance—experienced as confusion about one's originally assigned gender and sex. Taking stock by making identity comparisons about the originally assigned gender and sex and other alternatives leads to a revelatory moment, where one discovers transgenderism that enables reimagination of a more accurate gender identity. Initial identity confusion about one's own transgender status, usually sorted out through exposure and comparison with an existing group of transgender-identified others, eventually leads to tolerance and eventual acceptance of one's transgender identity. Although this process is rarely linear, for many transgender individuals it eventually leads to transition (though it is clarified that transition is defined and experienced in a multitude of ways). In the late stages of this model, transgender individuals integrate their original, suppressed gender identity with their previous sense of self, emerging proud and resolved to live authentically. This stage may be mediated by the effects of an inhospitable culture. As Devor (2004) noted, "Until such time as society at large achieves greater gender integration, the achievement and maintenance of identity pride of transpeople as a whole and as individuals will require continual effort and vigilance" (p. 65).

Another recent study (Morgan and Stevens, 2008), which examined the identity development of twelve transgender adults (identifying as female to male transgender) ages thirty-four to forty-nine, revealed that a sense of mind-body dissonance, or the sense that one's body did not conform to one's felt sense of her own gender, preceded any actual notion of transgender identity. Puberty was a time of acute discomfort, particularly as parents and others imposed expectations of dress and behavior on the participants, causing significant emotional distress. Affiliation with a BGLT community was helpful but insufficient, as noted by a student named Tyler: "I went off to college, and I thought, okay, maybe I'll meet a nice woman and I'll settle down. So then I met my current wife, except, it wasn't like a lesbian thing. We said, well, maybe we're dykes. But, that wasn't really it" (Morgan and Stevens, 2008, p. 592).

Although their efforts to proceed with transition were frequently stymied, especially in their early adult years, participants in this study eventually described reaching a breaking point, when they knew they could no longer hide in their assigned gender. The relentless output of energy required to adapt to a life of incoherence between one's known or felt self and the way one is viewed by the world became simply too much to bear. This emergence is the key to achieving a restored sense of wholeness; as noted by the authors, "Compromise and conformity only [delay] the achievement of comfort and acceptance that comes from being able to live outwardly and openly as their preferred gender" (Morgan and Stevens, 2008, p. 599).

These theories are helpful for expanding our understanding of the hurdles faced by transgender students in their quest to live as the gender they experience, but theories of identity development not centered in late adolescence can obscure the particularities of arriving at one's identity while in college, particularly for the 63 percent of college students who are between the ages of eighteen and twenty-five (U.S. Census Bureau, 2009). We then must extrapolate from these later adult reflections on transition, despite the fact that the initial exploration of gender identity is a common experience for transgender youth upon matriculating in college (Beemyn, 2003a; Pusch, 2003). In addition to our limited understanding of how they develop and what developmentally instigative characteristics (Evans and others, 2010) look like for this population, we have a very limited sense of what college means for them, during as well as after their years on campus.

To better conceptualize the path transgender students follow in their coming out, Bilodeau (2005a) has suggested that a life-span model of sexual identity development is useful for analyzing transgender identity as it unfolds in college; D'Augelli's model of six developmental processes (1994a), as described in the previous chapter, offers a way of thinking about how transgender students come to understand and express gender nonconformity as a function of their own context, shaped by relationships with peers, family, and others. Bilodeau's case studies of two students' experiences at a midwestern university demonstrated a first step of exiting a traditionally gendered identity. Through observing others who identify as transgender and connecting with others at similar stages in self-realization, transgender students next move to developing a personal transgender identity—which may or may not include gender transition, as Bilodeau's participants expressed (2005a). In the third stage, developing a transgender social identity, connections with BGLT groups and advocating for trans inclusion within them appears to be a pivotal step, along with attending conferences and tapping into supportive friendships for sustenance.

Next comes disclosure to one's family as transgender by becoming a transgender offspring. Determining and expressing one's authentic, self-determined sexual identity in tandem with gender is the project of the next phase, developing a transgender intimacy status. Finally, in a full-circle culmination of the process of self-discovery, both students in Bilodeau's study entered a transgender community, experiencing a strong need to resist the societal oppression experienced as a result of being gender nonconforming.

The Challenge of Transphobia on Campus

Transgender students' visibility is increasing and, along with it, an awareness of the specific challenges faced by this population as they attempt to navigate their campus communities. Obstacles to full participation include actual and perceived threats to their safety, denial of their ability to self-identify in the classroom and cocurricular activities, and adverse mental and physical health effects stemming from generalized oppression faced in the dominant culture (Beemyn, 2003b; Bilodeau, 2005a; Lees, 1998; Mallon, 1999; McKinney, 2005). Students attempting to live authentically as transgender, in addition to assessing and negotiating these challenges, must frequently do so without identifiable role models and thus are frequently cast in the role of pioneer on their campus.

Although the nature of the college experience for transgender students varies greatly depending on factors such as their numbers at any one institution, its geographical location, and the availability and access to resources and support, transphobia appears to be manifested in at least three typical ways in the college environment: genderism (Bilodeau, 2005a, 2005b; Wilchins, 2002), harassment and the potential (and actual) violence committed against transgender students, and exacerbation of mental health effects of gender-based oppression.

Genderism

Many of the challenges faced by transgender students revolve around the fact that colleges and universities practice a rigid and codified process of enforcing binary (male and female) gender norms known as "genderism." This practice, originally defined by transgender activist Wilchins (2002) as the ways that individuals, institutions, and society at large both subtly and overtly reinforce a system of binary genders, requires that individuals conform to this binary to succeed in these institutions. Colleges and universities are particularly prone to the practice of genderism, and, in a multitude of ways affecting students from the moment of matriculation until graduation, a clear expectation is communicated that students are ever only male or female and that they must exhibit gender identities coherent with their biological sex (Bilodeau 2005a, 2005b).

Everyday activities like requiring students to identify as male or female on admissions forms, dividing students into male and female designations on athletic teams, and centering roommate matching for new students based on a male or female identity, while considered normal ways of categorizing students in college, have profound implications for students in gender transition or who prefer to live outside the gender binary altogether. Far from being a benign and simplistic way of organizing student life, researchers have argued that "genderism is an ideology that reinforces the negative evaluation of gender non-conformity or an incongruence between sex and gender. It is a cultural belief that perpetuates negative judgments of people who do not present as a stereotypical man or woman. Those who are genderist believe that people who do not conform to sociocultural expectations of gender are pathological" (Hill and Willoughby, 2005, p. 534). Students attempting to navigate college from inside the binary and live outside it (or in transition) experience stress as the "nonnormativity" of their identities is relentlessly reinforced.

Harassment and Violence

The Oscar-winning 1999 film *Boys Don't Cry* depicts the life and brutal murder of Brandon Teena, a young transgender man who was viciously attacked by two men in his community (Peirce, 1999). Throughout the film, Brandon's previous female identity is known to the audience but not to those who murdered him, and discovery of his gender enrages these men as they come to terms with Brandon's true identity. Brandon's life is symbolic of the fact that transgender young people who dare to live authentically are at elevated risk of experiencing various forms of harassment, sexual and physical abuse, and even murder (Bilodeau, 2005a; Henning-Stout, James, and Macintosh, 2000; Kosciw and Diaz, 2006; Wyss, 2004).

Beemyn and Rankin's survey (forthcoming) of 3,474 transgender people revealed that 60 percent of respondents sometimes or often feared for their physical safety; 44 percent of those age twenty-two and under had experienced harassment, including derogatory remarks, damage to property, threats of violence, and actual violence. These results are corroborated in Grant and others' study (2011) of the experiences of 7,500 transgender people of all ages and backgrounds, which revealed that 78 percent of those who expressed a transgender identity or gender nonconformity while in kindergarten through twelfth grade experienced harassment. Additionally, a full third had endured some form of physical assault, and 12 percent had experienced sexual abuse (Grant and others, 2011). Of those who had been harassed, about 6 percent had been expelled, and about 15 percent had dropped out of primary or high school or college. Although peers were the primary source of this behavior, teachers and staff members were also responsible for harassment; one-third of respondents reported harassment by teachers or other staff members, 5 percent reported physical assault by teachers or staff, and 3 percent reported sexual assault by teachers or staff (Grant and others, 2011).

How does this harassment and violence manifest on the college campus? In a national survey of 5,149 respondents conducted in spring 2009 (Rankin, Weber, Blumenfeld, and Frazer, 2010), 695 students, faculty, and staff did not identify within the gender binary (in other words, they identified as being on the transmasculine spectrum, on the transfeminine spectrum, or as otherwise gender nonconforming). Of those who identified as being on the transmasculine spectrum, 39 percent had experienced harassment; 38 percent of transfeminine respondents had, and 31 percent of those who were gender nonconforming in other ways had experienced harassment. This rate of mistreatment was nearly double that of gender-conforming respondents to the survey, many of whom were also bisexual, gay, or lesbian. The types of harassment these respondents described ranged from subtle forms such as being deliberately left out or excluded or being singled out as a resident authority, being stared at, being targets of graffiti, being harassed in the context of a class, and being intimidated or bullied. Fears of social isolation, fearing the possibility of receiving a poor grade in a course, or being afraid for one's safety were the most commonly reported effects of this maltreatment. Gender-nonconforming respondents of color in this survey were significantly more likely to experience harassment than their peers who were not gender nonconforming, and both groups were more likely to experience harassment than white respondents of all gender identities (Rankin, Weber, Blumenfeld, and Frazer, 2010).

In addition to verbal and physical harassment directed toward transgender people, sexual abuse, known to be particularly prevalent in college women (Fisher, Cullen, and Turner, 2000) is also experienced in disproportionate numbers by transgender people: as many as 50 percent have experienced sexual or other forms of physical assault by a partner (Courvant and Cook-Daniels, 1998). As noted in a recent national survey of student mental health, 32 percent of transgender students, compared with 21 percent of nontrans students, reported experiencing unwanted sexual contact (Center for Collegiate Mental Health, 2010).

Hate-based incidents, sometimes also called bias incidents, are not uncommon in campus settings where transgender students are becoming more visible, active, and vocal about their unmet needs and the ways that discrimination affects their experiences on campus (Beemyn, 2003a; Nakamura, 1998). College campuses act as sites of replication and perpetuation of dominant cultural norms, and it is common for transgression of these norms to be met with resistance and even hostility. A recent attack on a transgender graduate student at California State University–Long Beach, perpetrated by a person who forced the student into a bathroom stall and carved the word "it" into his chest, is a painfully vivid example of a hate crime directed at a transgender college student (Fishman, 2010). Given the urgency of addressing violence and harassment toward transgender individuals, different approaches have been employed to respond. Reflecting the current stance of transgender advocacy organizations, Beemyn (2003a) calls for zero tolerance for harassment of transgender students and for implementing policies that are made widely available and known to all members of the campus community. Zero tolerance implies that students who harass or otherwise harm transgender students would be immediately sanctioned and that this sanctioning would affirm the prioritizing of transgender students' safety.

Schlosser and Sedlacek (2001) outline a different strategy—one of taking time to evaluate hate incidents, place them in context, and deal with the incident "through ongoing dialogue and education" (p. 26). This approach, devoid of clear accountability for offenders, suggests that these incidents are in fact most appropriately viewed as moments where learning about diversity can be affirmed rather than examples of ways that violation of transgender students' rights will not be allowed to flourish. The philosophy of this approach is reflected in the idea that "incidents will continue to occur, despite the best prevention programs" and emphasizes "turn[ing] a negative incident of hatred into a positive learning opportunity" (p. 27). In so doing, the discourse of accountability and consequences is virtually absent from the consideration of how these incidents might best be handled.

The conundrum exhibited in these two differential messages is attributable to the ambivalence felt by many on college campuses when free speech is theoretically threatened but then is problematized by the reality that hate speech often inhibits the ability of oppressed minorities (such as transgender and other gender-variant people) to their right to learn safely and without threat of harm. It is possible to balance both considerations and to envision an approach that combines zero tolerance of transgender harassment with dialogue and learning, but to be maximally supportive of transgender students, accountability must also be present and unquestioned, especially in situations where a student's safety or well-being were jeopardized by peer behavior.

Exacerbation of Mental Health Effects

"The registrar's office practically laughed me out the door when I requested my name be changed on my college records. . . . I ended up having to file papers for a legal name change with a lawyer. . . . More than one student has gotten up from their desk and moved when I've sat next to them. One day as I walked to class, minding my own business, a guy pointed at me and laughed out loud. . . . The stress of continually dealing with these sorts of difficulties . . . caught up with me. . . . My body and soul needed a break" (Rogers, 2000, pp. 17–18). As echoed in these words of one transgender student at a large public institution, the compound effects of genderism, harassment, and violence against transgender people—whether manifested physically or psychologically—can be enormously detrimental to the growth and development of transgender adolescents. The daily toll of attempting to live in the binary gender framework and to manage the perceptions of peers, faculty, and others with whom trans students interact on campus can have negative effects, including depression, anxiety, inability to focus on pursuing one's life goals, and a profound sense of isolation. Navigating a culture that does not support or encourage gender nonconformity in addition to pursuing academic work and other activities, particularly without easily identifiable role models, can be an exhausting endeavor.

Unsurprisingly, transgender students exhibit compromised mental health as a result of these daily challenges. Treatment for transgender college students experiencing the adverse mental health effects of genderism has long been overshadowed by the belief, endorsed in the professional practice literature of physicians until the mid-1990s, that transgender people are innately disordered and in need of clinical intervention and a cure (Feinberg, 1996; Money, 1994; Strassberg, Roback, Cunningham, and Larson, 1979). In an effort to cope with the stresses of living in a culture typified by genderism, self-cutting, restrictive eating, and substance abuse are typical maladaptive coping mechanisms (Burgess, 1999; Mallon, 1999; Pazos, 1999). A recent national survey of student mental health indicates that, regardless of whether or not they seek treatment for a mental health condition, compared with their nontransgender peers, transgender students are twice as likely to report practicing self-harming behaviors, are twice as likely to have considered suicide, and are three times more likely to have attempted suicide on at least one occasion (Center for Collegiate Mental Health, 2011).

The Resilience of Transgender Students

It is critical to understand that although transgender students appear to be at greater risk for the negative health behaviors associated with coping with transphobia, they should not be presumed to be mentally unstable. In the earlier literature, the predominant subtext associated with understanding transgender students and addressing their needs tended to position these students as troubled, psychologically and interpersonally. As Marine (2009) has observed, case studies (Flowers, 2000; Nakamura, 1998) and essays (Carter, 2000; Lees, 1998) that included transgender students as actors emphasize the sense that transgender students feel chronically misunderstood, are under siege by their peers (BGL and straight alike), are confrontational in ways that may be disproportionate to the actual wrongs they experience on campus, and are struggling immensely with acceptance of self as well as acceptance by others. Students in these situations are portrayed as inexplicably hostile or dramatically vulnerable, and their relationships with others are precarious if not nonexistent.

For example, Nakamura (1998) noted, "Many transgender students are ashamed of their status and hate the public gaze that is cast on them. As a result they might be unwilling to report [hate] incidents because they don't want to cause more trouble" (p. 182). The theme of transgender students' college experience as laden with traumatic moments is reflected in the way that Nakamura (1998) also describes transsexuality as "a long-term process with many short-term crises" (p. 186).

To be fair, this assumption is partly a reflection of the fact that transgender students certainly can and do face significant struggles for acceptance on campus and that these exercises and essays are undoubtedly designed to emphasize the serious implications for transgender students of transphobia. The constant representation of transgender students as troubled, however, reinforces the persistent belief that these students are in some way mentally unstable or, worse, mentally ill. Although the psychiatric profession continues to stigmatize gender nonconformity by categorizing it as a disorder (American Psychiatric Association, 2000), this mind-set is subtly reinforced when few or no examples of transgender students' resilience are noted. While some transgender students may in fact be in deep turmoil regarding their gender identity, particularly at the beginning of their process of exploration, others (for example, Fried, 2000; Gray, 2000; Rabideau, 2000) exhibit abundant evidence that they have become stable in their sense of self as they moved through their college years and are inclined to pursue activism, public recognition of their community concerns, and social and institutional change. From these stories, we begin to understand that their personal struggles are one component, but not the entire picture, of transgender students' college experience.

Although empirical evidence documenting the experiences, challenges, and related developmental milestones of transgender students is limited, literature describing establishment of effective student services for transgender students is more available, particularly literature that includes directives for the larger umbrella group of BGLT students. Transgender students' needs, and the services and policies designed to meet them, are an important facet of colleges and universities' extension of inclusion for this population.

Transgender Students' Needs and Services

Thanks to the recent explosion of interest in documenting transgender students' needs, colleges and universities now have a clear mandate to proceed with improving the campus climate with respect to transgender students' presence. Given what is known about the struggles faced by these students, what should colleges and universities do to ensure that transgender students' concerns are addressed? As a beginning, several scholars have indicated specific ways that educational institutions can most appropriately support transgender students:

Educational programming for students that addresses the identities, needs, and concerns of transgender students (Beemyn, 2005; Beemyn, Domingue, Pettitt, and Smith, 2005; Bilodeau, 2005b, 2007; Nakamura, 1998),

Training of staff and faculty to understand and support transgender students (Beemyn, 2005; Beemyn, Domingue, Pettitt, and Smith, 2005; Bilodeau, 2007; Henning-Stout, James, and Macintosh, 2000; Wyss, 2004),

Creation of trans-focused support services in combination with lesbian, gay, and bisexual student services or as stand-alone programs (Beemyn, 2005; Beemyn, Curtis, Davis, and Tubbs, 2005; Beemyn, Domingue, Pettitt, and Smith, 2005; Bilodeau, 2005b, 2007; Henning-Stout, James, and Macintosh, 2000; Rankin, 2004; Renn, 2007),

Available and appropriately trained mental health support professionals to cope with the effects of transphobia and genderism (Beemyn, Domingue, Pettitt, and Smith, 2005; McKinney, 2005; Namaste, 2000; Wyss, 2004),

Access to flexible residence hall rooming arrangements, athletic facility locker rooms, and campus bathroom configurations that are appropriate for each student's self-determined gender identity (Beemyn, 2005; Beemyn,

Curtis, Davis, and Tubbs, 2005; Beemyn, Domingue, Pettitt, and Smith, 2005; Bilodeau, 2007),

The ability to modify official campus documents and records, including name and gender changes (Beemyn, 2003a, 2005; Beemyn, Curtis, Davis, and Tubbs, 2005; Beemyn, Domingue, Pettitt, and Smith, 2005; Bilodeau, 2007),

Increased attention to developing transgender-specific models of student development (Bilodeau, 2005b; Bilodeau and Renn, 2005), and

Access to trans-specific medical care, including assistance for those who wish to medically or surgically transition their sex (Beemyn, 2003a, 2005; Beemyn, Curtis, Davis, and Tubbs, 2005; Bilodeau, 2005a, 2007; McKinney, 2005).

As Marine (2009) has observed, some literature calls for an outright conversion of what some researchers identify as an oppressive binary gender system to one that embraces a more fluid, malleable, and self-created gender identity (Bilodeau, 2007; Bornstein, 1994; Butler, 1990; Chess, Kafer, Quizar, and Richardson, 2004; Wyss, 2004), while other assessments of the merits of this approach have argued that such changes should be approached cautiously because of their unknown impact on the continuing struggle for advancement of women's status on campus (Bilodeau, 2005b).

In light of these recommendations, the literature to date contains a clear mandate for higher education environments to be structured in such a way as to empower transgender students to navigate and effectively use campus resources (Beemyn, 2003a; Bilodeau and Renn, 2005; Nakamura, 1998). Because their situation is the least well understood of all BGLT-identified students, three specific recommendations for building communities of support for transgender students follow:

Recommendation 1: Transgender students are a distinct group with an identity worthy of focused study. To understand the uniqueness of transgender college students, researchers and practitioners alike ought to commit to learning about their history and culture and understanding their uniquely configured student, activist, and support communities. To work effectively with transgender students, student affairs professionals and faculty alike must first advance their own learning about this population, whose history has often been made invisible or co-opted by the history of gays and lesbians (Namaste, 2000; Stryker, 2008). Many professionals who are otherwise knowledgeable about bisexual, gay, and lesbian rights movements and history may be surprised to learn that transgender community leaders were pivotal in spearheading the Stonewall riots (Duberman, 1993).

It is important that student affairs practitioners who are not transgender make a commitment to learn the terminology and pronouns ("hir" and "ze," for example) preferred by trans individuals and to know what questions are appropriate (How do you identify in terms of your gender identity?) and not appropriate (Have you had sex change surgery? Do you plan to?) to ask in efforts to be meaningfully allied. Cisgender student affairs professionals can learn this information relatively easily by familiarizing themselves with local, regional, and national transgender activist organizations and the extensive array of information available through their vast network of Internet sites and communities. Becoming acquainted with this community, distinct and apart from BGL student concerns, demonstrates commitment to supporting transgender student development.

Recommendation 2: Support transgender college students in the use of strategies and tools to connect with other trans people and to manage and reduce oppression in their lives. Studying any youthful population solely from the perspective of deficits is an ineffective and one-dimensional approach and one that is no longer considered sound practice in the study of human development (Scales, Leffert, and Lerner, 1999). Limited in number but extremely informative in their depth and breadth, transgender student narratives and observational research enable those in positions of power to glimpse the struggles of their lives on campus as well as their remarkable internal and communal assets. Closer inspection of direct student experience can invaluably inform the development of best practices for transgender students (Beemyn, 2003a).

The narratives featured in *Out and About on Campus* (Howard and Stevens, 2000) are diverse in scope and experience but feature common themes of resilience. Far from fitting the aforementioned stereotype of terminally conflicted and asocial, Rogers (2000) describes not only coming out and transitioning at a large, rural state university in the Midwest but also identifying supportive peers and returning to college at age thirty after a long absence while working to support himself through school. Gray (2000) describes the travails he faced as he braved the judgment and harassment of peers for the self-affirming act of wearing a dress to class on a regular basis, reflecting that "some people claim that I cross-dress as an immature way of getting attention. But if everyone stopped paying attention, I would still do it (and it would be so much easier)" (p. 87).

Assessing (probably accurately) that he could not fully explore his cross-dressing identity on his rural midwestern campus, Fried (2000) took advantage of a foreign study program opportunity to travel to Holland and in so doing experienced true liberation in a new culture, evolving into a more comfortable version of himself. In each of these student's lives, the perceived fragility and vulnerability dissolves and a sense of these students' strength, creativity, and resolve takes its place.

Resiliency echoes through the most comprehensive study of transgender college students to date, the dissertation of Rob Pusch at Syracuse University. Pusch (2003) studied the activity of ten college students, diverse in gender identity and college environments and all identified as transgender, through an Internet relay chat room. Seven male-to-female and three female-to-male students, at different stages in their transition, took part in the community observation, a community in which Pusch was also a participant. In light of the regular oppression they faced, these students' coping behaviors included accessing the online community to process through experiences and gain support for various decisions regarding physical presentation and other gender modifications and accessing mentoring from older trans individuals who had faced similar questions. The participants were clear that they did not wish to be viewed as abnormal and experienced frustration with the almost constant judgment and pathology applied to their gender expression decisions. Transgender students in this study first found community through reading about trans identities, then by attempting to connect with others online, and finally in person, a sequence it would be helpful to remember when working to serve the needs of these students. Additionally, the students in the study gave eloquent voice to the marginalization they experience in BGL student communities and social locations, affirming the need to ensure that BGLT student organizations and centers are regularly reviewed for the extent to which they are trans inclusive.

Recommendation 3: Work with transgender students and their allies to identify and reduce the effects of genderism on campus. Perhaps the most important and stress-reducing initiative that those with influence over higher education policy and practice can take is to learn how to most effectively identify and act to reduce the effects of genderism (Bilodeau, 2005a, 2005b) on the college campus. Genderism, as noted previously, can and does take many forms, from the material reality of being assigned a same-sex roommate to the indignity of being asked to enter a single-gender bathroom when instead a single-stall bathroom with no gender designation would be most appropriate. Student affairs practitioners of all genders can be instrumental in thinking about the ways that their institution constructs opportunities as well as requirements for students in a way that proscribes gender as solely binary. Asking questions about the necessity of assigning gender to facilities opens up space for flexibility. Wondering aloud about the merits of assigning gender to college or university traditions and rituals creates possibility for those who have consistently felt excluded. And although some aspects of collegiate life—intercollegiate athletics, for example—are undergoing revolutionary shifts in thinking about sex and gender (Griffin and Carroll, 2010), it cannot be underestimated to what extent smaller, more incremental changes matter too.

Conclusion

Moving into the twenty-first century, student affairs professionals and faculty in higher education are being asked to become more knowledgeable about the ways that differing student populations are understood and effectively served. Although understanding student development as a relatively uniform phenomenon has served student affairs well for the first half century of its existence, it is arguable that costs are associated with doing so for students who do not fit the typical profile and experiences of undergraduates who have lived their lives with a stable and unchanging sense of their own gender identity.

Although terminology is important to a sense of inclusion, simply adding "transgender" to arguments for the essential concerns of sexual orientation minorities on campus does little to combat the invisibility of transgender students' specific needs. Beemyn (2003a) makes the case effectively for why consistently subsuming transgender students' concerns under the heading of BGLT restricts higher education professionals' understanding of trans specificity in ways that can be harmful to these students. For best practice information to be relevant to the issues of transgender students, their experiences must be studied more specifically, and researchers and practitioners alike must exhibit familiarity with their narratives in ways that are more than symbolically inclusive. Transgender people have a rich and storied history of resistance and self-definition, yet many who conduct and disseminate research on queer college experiences are not conversant with the language, politics, and community values of the transgender population. And this lack of knowledge may in turn trickle down to development of programs and services: As one BGLT resource center coordinator helpfully noted, "We have the word transgender in our title, but we aren't very good about including transgender themes in the things we do" (Rabideau, 2000, p. 173).

Today, the movement for transgender rights has advanced—if not secured nationally—many important agendas, including the right of transgender people to partner, raise children, seek (and retain) employment, and have protection from police harassment (Frye, 2000). But many challenges to their full personhood remain, forty years after Sylvia Rivera led the march out of the Stonewall Inn, demanding the rights that have yet to arrive. Along with American society as a whole, higher education must answer the call to respond more meaningfully to the full inclusion of transgender students.

The BGLT Campus Resource Center

Our work is to create a community feeling that will bring a homophile movement into being.

—SIR's first president, William Beardemphl,
quoted in Schlager, 1998, p. 49

A S STUDENTS WHO ARE BGLT have become increasingly more visible and vocal on American college and university campuses, so too has higher education adapted to create structures needed to promote their development. Since the early 1970s, the typical response to the question "What do BGLT students in higher education need?" has been "a center." The allocation of physical space, financial and other material resources, and, in many cases, the presence of professional leadership, has enabled the campus BGLT center (or as will be explored later in this chapter, often known as the queer center) to become a prominent fixture on (to date) 190 college and university campuses across the country (Consortium of Higher Education LGBT Resource Professionals, 2011).

Campus BGLT centers reflect the history of the larger movement for queer visibility, rooted in the belief that through solidarity and togetherness, progress can be made toward securing the rights and safety of all. Originally, that solidarity was found in the camaraderie established in the gay bar, which functioned both as a place to congregate and a kind of hiding place. According to Clendinen and Nagourney (1999), gay bars pre-Stonewall "were in windowless buildings, or buildings whose windows had been covered or blacked out, and whose entries went through a solid door, usually with a peephole guarded by bouncers" (p. 17). Personal risk of harassment, whether by police, antigay activists, or even just passersby, was a real and present danger for those choosing to socialize in these spaces. As a once-hidden subculture of marginalized individuals began to emerge and publicly organize for social change, community spaces appropriated for the flourishing of queer life included meeting halls, coffeehouses, and eventually community centers (Katz, 1992; Stryker and Van Buskirk, 1996). Unsurprisingly, BGLT activists in large urban areas were the first to seek out and claim space "above ground," where they could come together and foment revolution.

The Society for Individual Rights (SIR), a San Francisco–based homophile organization, founded the first center for BGLT people and their concerns in 1966 (Schlager, 1998). The Los Angeles Gay and Lesbian Center, the oldest continuously operating community center for BGLT people and their concerns, was founded in 1971; it originally focused on providing for the most basic needs of the community, including housing, employment assistance, and health care. The organization secured public funding in 1974 (Schlager, 1998). After becoming the first BGLT-focused organization in the United States to achieve 501(c)3 status, today the center (which has expanded its mission to serve bisexual and transgender people as well) has 250 full-time employees and a budget of $30 million, making it the largest and best funded of all national centers (Batza, 2007). A thriving National Association of Lesbian and Gay Community Centers, now 150 members strong, was also founded in 1994 to connect BGLT community centers and in so doing build their resources and capacity to serve the needs of the community (Hunter, 2007b).

The First BGLT Campus Resource Centers: Their Founding and Purposes

As described earlier, students began organizing around BGLT student issues in the late 1960s as a result of the energy emanating immediately before and after the Stonewall riots and related political actions of the time. The first known space now called a campus resource center (Sanlo, 2000) for BGLT student rights and interests was founded at the University of Michigan in 1971 and was named the "Lesbian–Gay Male Programs Office" (Schlager, 1998, p. 211).

The office was co-coordinated by a woman (Cynthia Gair) and a man (Jim Toy), who were first part time then full time in their roles (Toy, 2008). Perhaps owing to the early establishment of a BGLT center, Michigan was one of the first universities to add the words "sexual orientation" to its list of identity categories about which discrimination was prohibited (Sanlo, Rankin, and Schoenberg, 2002).

Today, according to the Consortium of Higher Education LGBT Resource Professionals (2011), approximately 190 colleges and universities, ranging from large public land-grant colleges to small private liberal arts colleges and everywhere in between, offer their students a professionally staffed and funded BGLT campus resource center. In the first decade of mobilization to form queer campus resource centers, most were located in large public state universities (such as Pennsylvania State University and the University of South Carolina). In the 1980s, again as a result of student activism, more private colleges christened space for BGLT student support (Sanlo, Rankin, and Schoenberg, 2002). The first, and to date only, community college center for BGLT students was founded in Denver in 1993 (Ivory, 2005). Although movement toward formation of centers has been steady, attrition has also occurred: four colleges and universities have eliminated their existing staff position for BGLT student life since 2005 (Consortium of Higher Education LGBT Resource Professionals, 2011).

Particularly when thinking about the importance of dedicated social space in the advancement of social movements, beginnings matter. In the words of Tamara Cohen, who worked on the establishment of the GLBT Center at the University of Florida, "some of the challenge in starting a new program is letting the university know you exist" ("Building a GLBT Center from the Ground Up," 2005, p. 1). Understanding the genesis of BGLT centers was the focus of a study conducted by Ritchie and Banning (2001). Capturing the narratives of how these centers were founded and grew in their early years, they determined that two patterns typified the founding of these centers: that they were founded as the end result of a university-endorsed task force or as a response to incident(s) of visible harassment or discrimination toward the BGLT community.

Resistance to and support for their formation played equally important roles in defining their missions; founders employed creative and diverse strategies and tactics to counteract those who objected to their presence. Each had a distinctive story, but taken as a whole, the themes of resistance and persistence characterized the centers' start in this study. Ronni Sanlo, a long-time advocate for BGLT campus resource centers and services in higher education, observed that "there is no packaged, step-by-step process in creating an LGBT presence on your campus" but that conducting a campus climate survey, developing recommendations directly from the results, and implementing these recommendations with faculty, staff, and student collaboration is a sound way to begin ("Setting Up an LGBT Center on Your Campus," 2006, p. 1).

Typically, student activists have played a significant role in the creation of queer resource centers. The GLBT Center at the University of Minnesota, founded after a series of homophobic incidents on campus as one aspect of a five-point plan to address the marginality of BGLT life, is emblematic of how the securing of space, funding, and human resources can result from sustained queer student organizing on campus. Following a successful campaign by students, the university's president appointed a subcommittee on lesbian, gay, and bisexual concerns that exhaustively studied the state of affairs at the University of Minnesota for three years. According to Zemsky (1996), the center's "effectiveness owes much to its official university status and specific mandate to conduct a university-wide study. It was also significant that the committee was predominantly comprised of openly GLBT students, faculty, and staff, as well as a cadre of vocal heterosexual allies, in a powerful example of coalition building" (p. 209).

The founding of BGLT campus resource centers at state universities frequently entails securing financial support from student fees, and thus objections may be made on the grounds that some in the state do not wish to support such centers with tax dollars. Oregon State University (OSU) was the site of this kind of debate in 2001, when student activists faced down opposition to secure $7,000 in funding to establish their first center (Ryan, 2005). Fifteen years later, after numerous incremental expansions of programs and services, the OSU center requested and received a $120,000 budget, in part to refurbish and equip the space to serve the growing community of BGLT students. Significant and protracted efforts to demonstrate need and assess capacity were essential to this center's growth in the face of some public disapproval for BGLT rights and visibility on the campus (Bafico, 2006; Blake, 2006). Centers located at private institutions, sometimes situated in spacious and lavishly adorned freestanding buildings, communicate the progress made since their founding. Regarding the center at the University of Pennsylvania's prominent location on campus, the architect who built the space commented that "there's something rich about a gay and lesbian center at Penn being one of these classic back buildings that represents . . . that the kids are quite out and visible on campus" (Sokol, 2003, p. 129). The symbolism of BGLT student life's moving from the margins to the very heart of the campus at this vaunted institution thus advances queer students' sense of having a seat at the table to both form and inform Penn's traditions in the future.

BGLT Centers Today: Their Purposes and Roles

Like community-based centers, BGLT campus resource centers often reflect the unique histories, purposes, and priorities of their particular campus setting while sharing a common purpose: ensuring the vitality and flourishing of students of minority sexual orientations and gender identities. To understand exactly how this transpires, it is helpful to examine the current status, functions, and foci of BGLT student programs and services on American college campuses today, to examine the values and goals of professional training in queer students services, and to consider the leadership and histories of the professional associations that support these centers. What do those who are sometimes called "gays for pay" (and the centers or offices where they work) bring to the project of enabling BGLT students to thrive on the college campus today?

Like many other functional areas in student affairs, BGLT campus resource centers and services are typically tailored specifically to the needs of that particular institution, and those needs may fluctuate depending on the campus climate, recent events in the local community or state, and trends or patterns with national reverberation. Recent research about these centers (Beemyn, 2002; Browning and Walsh, 2002; "Building a GLBT Center from the Ground Up," 2005; Ryan, 2005; Sanlo, Rankin, and Schoenberg, 2002; Schlager, 1998; Zemsky, 1996) indicate four major functions and seven major services and purposes of BGLT campus resource centers (Exhibit 2).

EXHIBIT 2

Major Functions, Services, and Purposes of BGLT Campus Resource Centers

Function	Service	Purpose
Assessment/evaluation	Assessment of campus climate for BGLT students, faculty, and staff.	To determine needs and concerns of students, faculty, staff, and the allied community to develop targeted programs.
Counseling/support	Professional support services for individual students questioning their gender, sexual orientation, or both and those experiencing homo-, bi-, or transphobia and related harassment on campus.	To enhance students' access to information and resources, with the goal of reducing the negative effects of homo-, bi-, and transphobia.
	Training and supervision of peer counseling programs and other peer resources for students exploring BGLT identities.	To empower BGLT and allied students; to affirm identities through visible, accessible sources of peer support.
	Mentoring (both informal, through one-on-one consultation, and formal, through a structured program) of BGLT students.	To empower and support BGLT and allied students through connection with seasoned community members who can assist in strategizing about needs and concerns.
Education	Development and implementation of educational programs about bisexual, gay, lesbian, and transgender identities.	To promote the visibility of BGLT lives, histories, and politics and in so doing create a supportive climate for BGLT individuals.
Advocacy	Development and implementation of a response mechanism to hate or bias crimes.	To develop a swift, meaningful response mechanism for BGLT-related incidents that deters their occurrence.
	Advocacy for changes in policy and practice (such as gender-neutral housing, the inclusion of BGLTs in nondiscrimination policy, safe zone programs, and so on).	To adapt college or university environmental assets to needs of the BGLT population.

As described in the Exhibit, the seven major services can be grouped under four headings: assessment/evaluation, counseling/support, education, and advocacy. Although the degree to which these services are undertaken varies depending on institution, location, and history, the beginning point is assessment. Directors, along with advisory boards and other staff of BGLT centers, center their energies on the determination of needs in the three other areas, followed by implementation of programs and services to address those needs (Beemyn, 2002).

BGLT Students and Campus Climate Assessment

Assessment is an important feature in BGLT campus centers' ability to successfully implement programs and services targeted to the needs of students (Rankin and Hanson, 2011). Without well-developed mechanisms to determine the numbers, identities, and specific concerns of BGLT students on a specific campus, the development of programs that meaningfully serve their needs can be elusive (Schueler, Hoffman, and Peterson, 2009). Eyermann and Sanlo (2002) have demonstrated some of the complexities entailed in capturing accurate data about the numbers of students in various and specific BGLT identities, including the challenges of asking students to claim an identity of heterosexual, gay, lesbian, and bisexual without defining the meaning of those terms as well as the differences yielded when instead researchers inquire about students' identities and attractions.

To ascertain the lived realities of BGLT students at any given institution, data collected must extend beyond a census. Campus climate assessments—extensive multidimensional inquiries into the daily perceptions and environment for BGLT students—provide the most meaningful opportunities for analysis. Campus climate, defined as the "current attitudes, behaviors and standards, and practices of employees and students of an institution" is a comprehensive way to think about the environment that circumscribes students' everyday experiences (Rankin and Reason, 2008, p. 264). Campus climate measurement tools take a variety of forms, including campuswide surveys, focus groups, interviews, and open discussion forums (Rankin, 2003, 2005; Sanlo, Rankin, and Schoenberg, 2002). The goal of conducting campus climate assessments is to ascertain the degree to which BGLT-identified members of the community experience negative effects of homo-, bi-, and transphobia and the extent to which such experiences hamper or impede their daily participation in the community. Services and programs developed from the specific indicators of community members' experiences can thus be tailored to address these needs and, if conducted carefully, can be replicated over time. Institutions that undertake campus climate assessments with rigor are then well positioned to enter into a strategic planning process to ensure the relevance of programs and services provided over time. As noted by the director of the University of Pennsylvania's LGBT Center, "This endeavor represents another step in our growth and development. It will help us to know what we are doing now that we might be able to let go, what we are not doing now that should become a priority, and what sources we might be able to tap for support of future operations" (Sanlo, Rankin, and Schoenberg, 2002, p. 23).

Campus climate may look and feel different to students depending on their position as members and participants in various campus subcultures. Brown, Clarke, Gortmaker, and Robinson-Keilig (2004) studied student, faculty, and staff perceptions of BGLT campus climate at one institution using a diverse sample of both queer-identified and non-queer-identified participants and found that those for whom BGLT identity was personally salient perceived the campus climate more negatively and were (not surprisingly) more interested in and involved in BGLT-related educational activities, suggesting that majority (nonqueer students) might benefit from more exposure to the realities faced by their queer peers. A similar study comparing out students to those who concealed their BGLT identity from friends and faculty found that students who were openly BGLT were more likely to experience the campus climate as negative and at the same time were more involved in BGLT life on campus, suggesting that being open about one's BGLT identity might make one more sensitized to everyday harassment as well as more vulnerable to being targeted (Gortmaker and Brown, 2006).

In addition to gauging the perspectives of each individual institution's landscape for BGLT students, nationally conducted campus climate surveys offer insights that can be used to direct appropriate programs. Conducted in 2003, Rankin's national campus climate survey of one thousand students and nearly seven hundred faculty and staff at fourteen institutions across the nation revealed that 36 percent of BGLT undergraduates had experienced some form of harassment, mostly in the form of derogatory remarks (89 percent) made by other students (79 percent). Nearly half of respondents characterized their institution as homophobic, and 40 percent expressed a felt need to conceal their sexual orientation or nonnormative gender identity. In Rankin's study, asking broad-based questions about both experiences and effects yielded a rich picture of the kinds of experiences BGLT students have as well as the ways they affect their time on campus (Rankin, 2005).

Like the Rankin study in 2003, the Campus Pride *State of Higher Education for Lesbian, Gay, Bisexual and Transgender People* campus climate survey sought to capture the diverse experiences of students, faculty, and staff of various sexual and gender identities across a wide variety of institutions and other salient identities (Rankin, Weber, Blumenfeld, and Frazer, 2010). The 5,149 respondents to this survey, representing institutions in all fifty states, were asked about experiences with conduct that might interfere with their ability to live, work, and learn; their perceptions of overall campus climate, work unit climate, and classroom climate; and their individual and institutional responses to campus climate (Rankin, Weber, Blumenfeld, and Frazer, 2010). Also resonant with Rankin's 2003 study, 61 percent of BGLT students were targeted by harassment, 37 percent reported being stared at, and 36 percent were expected to serve as a resident authority regarding their identities—a rate twice as high, in each case, as their non-BGL peers. Other significant differences included the fact that 13 percent of BGLT students expressed fear for their physical safety, reported that they had been targeted as the victim of a crime (3 percent), or were targeted by physical violence (3 percent). In addition to behaviors experienced by BGLT students, the survey sought to understand the perceptions of climate respondents experienced and found that a significant number (20 percent) of BGLT-identified respondents were not comfortable with the overall campus climate, a percentage that was significantly higher among BGLT respondents of color.

In the increasingly competitive marketplace of higher education, how might colleges and universities assess their standing as BGLT-friendly institutions relative to other institutions? One metric of note is the LGBT-friendly campus climate index created by Campus Pride, a national organization promoting queer student visibility and empowerment (2011). The tool identifies fifty-four distinct items designed to measure institutional support in the realm of eight different categories (policy inclusion, support and institutional commitment, academic life, student life, housing, campus safety, counseling and health, and recruitment and retention). Because the tool is self-administered by a designated administrator, the possibility of misrepresenting one's institutional climate to portray favorable circumstances is real; thus, external evaluations of campus friendliness such as *The Advocate*'s guide to the most gay-friendly schools (Windmeyer, 2006) may be perceived to more accurately reflect an individual institution's landscape.

Although campus climate assessments are a critical first step in determining what action to take to improve the surroundings for BGLT students, they are not without problems: some have urged caution when considering undertaking them as they can trigger expectations for improvement that the college or university must invite only if administrators are prepared to address them (Hanson, 2010). Sound measurement of campus climate, as exemplified by institutional and national studies, matters to the isolation of common problems and concerns for BGLT students and development of meaningful solutions. Inhospitable climates for BGLT students impede, and interrupt, students' normal growth and development, in terms of their sexual orientation and gender identity (Wolf-Wendel, Toma, and Morphew, 2001; Wyss, 2004), their comfort and sense of belonging (Evans and Broido, 1999), and their overall cognitive, moral, and psychosocial development (Eddy and Forney, 2000; Silverschanz, Cortina, Konik, and Magley, 2007).

Center Leadership: A "New Profession" in Higher Education

BGLT resource centers on college and university campuses are sites of deep engagement by students, including allies. Finding a safe haven for exploration and affirmation of BGLT identities means that students envision, and drive, a great many of the activities at these centers. To harness and direct the energy of students and their allies, professional leadership—a part- or full-time staff person—invariably makes a difference in the productivity and reach of the center's work.

Intuitively, it seems reasonable to think that most who assume professional roles in BGLT resource centers identify as BGLT. They are prepared to take on these roles by virtue of their personal experience as well as professional training. Croteau and Lark (1995) assessed the climate of higher education student affairs for those who identify at bisexual, gay, or lesbian and found that most of these professionals are out as BGL to coworkers and others and that they are overwhelmingly satisfied with their jobs (75 percent). Nearly 80 percent were out to all or most of their coworkers, and 72 percent were satisfied with their degree of openness at work. Nonetheless, almost 60 percent had experienced discrimination at work, including verbal threats, graffiti, and unfair policies, and those who were most open were more likely to experience discrimination at work. Thus, those who are open are both more satisfied yet also more likely to experience discrimination at work—a complicated paradox. Directors of BGLT campus resource centers, as the most easily identifiable out members of any institution's staff, must thus contend with both the benefits and costs of their visibility.

What do we know about those who direct and lead the operations of BGLT centers? A survey of directors of institutions holding membership in the Consortium of Higher Education LGBT Resource Professionals (Sanlo, 2000) revealed that the majority of these personnel identify as female (56 percent), are an average of forty-one years of age, are 94 percent identified as homosexual, and identify racially as mostly white (88 percent). In terms of their qualifications, about half of the respondents hold a doctoral degree, the other half a master's degree. Seventy-eight percent of respondents locate their resource centers in student affairs, and others are situated with reporting lines to women's and gender centers. In terms of their motivations, center staff describe doing the work to improve students' college experiences in ways that their own had been lacking. One director links the work she does with other aspects of her identity, specifically her Judaism, saying "I believe in the importance of *tikkum olam,* repairing the world. I couldn't *not* do this work" (Sanlo, 2000, p. 492).

Other issues to be considered in defining the leadership of BGLT campus resource centers include ways to think about the merits of hiring a director from inside or outside the institution; identifying goals, an action plan to implement them, and evaluation rubrics; composing and appointing an advisory board; outlining a process for responding to critical incidents such as bias crimes; expanding and developing programs and services for BGLT staff and faculty; fundraising; and undertaking public relations and outreach to the community beyond the campus (Sanlo, Rankin, and Schoenberg, 2002).

Possessing significant personal commitment to the improvement of campus climate for BGLT students is an essential quality in a campus resource center director, particularly when encountering resistance to such change. Some obstacles that have been identified in the literature include other campus stakeholders' refusal to relinquish oversight to the director, micromanagement or territoriality of the center's budget process by stakeholders, and exclusion of the director from campus BGLT politics writ large (Sanlo, Rankin, and Schoenberg, 2002). Backlash from legislators resistant to supporting BGLT campus resource centers at state institutions can make employment at such centers precarious: directors may find themselves in and out of a job within one budget cycle ("Setting Up an LGBT Center on Your Campus," 2006).

To counter the personal and professional isolation experienced by directors of BGLT campus resource centers, the Consortium of Higher Education LGBT Resource Professionals, the unifying body of those who direct and otherwise staff BGLT resource centers, was founded in 1997. The association was formed after a group of BGLT campus resource center professionals came to realize that this group had specific interests and concerns and thus needed its own organization (Sanlo, Rankin, and Schoenberg, 2002). Among other efforts, the group sponsors professional development workshops and networking events at the major student affairs professional association conferences and operates a listserv for the sharing of information between and among staff at institutions across the country (Consortium of Higher Education LGBT Resource Professionals, 2011).

The Politics of BGLT Campus Resource Centers: Contested Territory

Although established to support a recognized student minority and to provide a fulcrum for mass exposure of the university community to BGLT identities, politics, and histories, BGLT campus resource centers are not without their detractors—and not without complexity. Talburt wrote about the contentious founding of one BGLT student resource center in *Thinking Queer: Sexuality, Culture, and Education* (2000). The establishment of the BGLT center at a large midwestern state university in the 1990s, as Talburt observed, was fraught with tension: although many at the pseudonymous Liberal U. supported the notion of pluralism and celebration of difference, many objected to the allocation of resources for support of this center. Ultimately, support was marshaled from a donor rather than from state tax funding, and the politics of the center's existence reinforced a particular frame of thinking about BGLT identity. Possessing or inhabiting a queer identity is a precursor to a set of personal problems, and to remedy it, institutions provide resources for resolution of these problems. According to Talburt, acknowledgment of "gay men and lesbians at Liberal U. is less acknowledgment of the construction of queerness per se or of the effects of institutionalized heterosexism and homophobia than it is an acknowledgment of individualized homosexual problems emanating from a pre-existing identity" (p. 75).

One area of contestation that offers rich insight into some of the generational and ideological shifts happening in and among these resources is in naming: the use, for example, of BGLT or some version thereof versus the more contemporary nomenclature of "queer resource centers." Several factors influence the naming of centers to support BGLT campus life: history (in the form of the name upon founding and the extent to which names change over time), the current politicization (or lack thereof) of centers, the relationship such centers have (or do not have) with academic programs in BGLT queer, women's, or feminist studies. Additionally, advocates establishing the center must contend with the reality that the institution may have obligations beyond its own walls—to a taxpaying public, to alumni and alumnae, or to a religious institution ("Setting Up an LGBT Center on Your Campus," 2006; Yoakam, 2006).

Often, name changes of centers to serve BGLT students represent a shift in thinking about who is the proper recipient of the services such centers provide. A recent name change for the lesbian, gay, bisexual, transgender, and ally student center at Western Washington University is a case in point. Student leaders there expressed the sense that "having any sort of acronym for a name is exclusive because we don't have enough room to include everyone. . . . We have a lot of people who use our office that aren't included in LGBT, so it was really about making this space more inclusive for everyone" (Welsh and Mohn, 2011). Rather than attaching the notion of queerness to any particular political perspective, the name is used to denote the broad swath of identities subsumed under the BGLT umbrella.

A different kind of transformation took place in 2004, when the formerly student-run (now professionally staffed) Oregon State University center for BGLT student life changed its name from "Queer Resource Center" to "Pride Center." According to an account in the student newspaper (Moser, 2004), *The Daily Barometer,* the word "queer" was chosen by the students who founded it because it served as both a meaningful and convenient umbrella term for the spectrum of identities it intended to serve—lesbian, gay, bisexual, transgender, queer, intersex, and allies. Other students felt, however, that the designation "queer" was unwelcoming and uncomfortable as it has historically been used as a pejorative. Although some felt that the name is the most globally inclusive signifier for the range of identities represented, others prioritized choosing a name that would appeal to a larger cross-section of the campus populace. According to one student activist involved with the center, "If this name offends anybody enough that they won't come to the center, then it needs to be changed" (Moser, 2004). The concept of a pride center, in keeping with the popular rhetoric of pride parades and celebrations, is uniquely affirming, signaling the focus on an empowerment function of the center for the campus. Today, the center has been renamed once again to the Office of LGBT Outreach and Services, reflecting a shift toward an orientation of providing service and hinting at the presence of a professionally led effort to support BGLT students.

BGLT campus resource centers vary with respect to how much different queer student subpopulations—women, students of color, or transgender students, for example—are involved. Westbrook (2009), after interviewing self-identified BGLT students, found a gender gap in participation in two different BGLT campus resource centers in California, caused in one case by "gender-blind organizing"—the lack of outreach leading to more female participation and ascension to leadership roles—perpetuated at the center. Students actively recruit new participants in center life from their own social networks; gay men tended thus to involve other gay men in creating the center's core base. This core base was then nurtured and developed to adopt leadership roles, resulting in a "patrimonial distribution of leadership support" (Westbrook, 2009, p. 383). Men fostered closeness with other men, then invested in those men's capacity for leadership, creating an almost unbroken pipeline of engagement and visibility in the center. In contrast, at the other institution, where women's involvement and leadership flourished, men and women alike had access to leadership development resources that empowered them to participate.

Considering the University of Minnesota's center, Zemsky (1996) also noted that some, particularly some women, may not feel comfortable connecting with resources through the LGBT center, depending on how the center defines itself and the extent to which that definition resonates with those who are seeking a "room of their own"—space explicitly dedicated to lesbians. Although all centers reviewed in the content analysis explicitly included transgender identity and support in their missions, full participation of transgender students and others in the community continues to remain a challenge. Once again, campus centers can look to preestablished community centers for guidance in this area; the LGBT Community Center in New York, despite its name, started an empowerment program for transgender community members in 1990, which focused on job placement and counseling, cultural competency for state agencies, and full-time trans-identified staff members (Warren, 2008).

Higher Education Student Affairs and BGLT Issues

Sexual orientation and gender identity are categories of identity that were scarcely recognized until the social upheaval post-Stonewall, which placed these issues front and center in the collective consciousness of many Americans. Higher education was no different from the culture at large in this respect; it was not until well after the emergence of homophile leagues in the late 1960s that student affairs as a field began to recognize its responsibility for understanding the specific developmental needs expressed by students of minority sexual orientations and gender identities.

To address the realities faced by this subpopulation, scholars have noted the importance of student affairs practitioners' taking a proactive approach to working with and supporting BGLT students (Croteau and Lark, 1995; Poynter and Washington, 2005; Sanlo, 1998; Wall and Evans, 2000; Zemsky and Sanlo, 2005). Specifically, student affairs professionals are called upon to enable students to take activist roles in promoting respect for BGLT identities (Porter, 1998; Watkins, 1998), to foster the creation of communities that are just and open (Boyer, 1990; Poynter and Washington, 2005), and to make additional efforts to support students for whom multiple aspects of identity such as minority racial identities are implicated (Abes, Jones, and McEwen, 2007; Pope, Reynolds, and Mueller, 2004; Poynter and Washington, 2005).

In keeping with the notion that possessing a knowledge base about students of different identities is imperative for ethical practice, both major student affairs professional organizations endorse learning about BGLT students and movements and offer professional development activities and community to enable this skill. As an arm of this commitment, the American College Personnel Association created a standing committee for LGBT awareness (with intentional reordering of the abbreviation) in 2002 (American College Personnel Association, 2007). Likewise, the National Association for Student Personnel Administrators (NASPA) also created a knowledge community for GLBT awareness in 2006 (formerly referred to as the LGBT Network), whose mission is to "provide avenues for both social and professional involvement. Knowledge Community activities allow for personal and professional growth, increased awareness and acceptance of gay, lesbian, bisexual and transgender professionals and students, and promote understanding of gay, lesbian, bisexual, and transgender professional and student needs" (National Association of Student Personnel Administrators, 2007).

Notably, the specific issues faced by transgender students appear to be on the contemporary radar of this organization, as evidenced by the activities of the Transgender Inclusion Committee; they include increased attention to providing gender-neutral bathroom facilities at the national conference, offering professional development programs, and continuously monitoring the progress of the organization around issues of transgender inclusion and leadership (National Association of Student Personnel Administrators, 2010). Although the emergence of a recognized body of BGLT-knowledgeable professionals in NASPA has been an important step for visibility of these issues in the organization, the shift to greater visibility has not been entirely easy for those in leadership roles. In her 2005 narrative about serving as first the chair of the LGBT Network and later the chair of the GLBT knowledge community, Albin noted the ways in which she felt vulnerable as one of a few openly lesbian women in a high-visibility leadership role in the organization; she also described her discouragement with the lack of openly GBLT role models among senior student affairs professionals (Albin and Dungy, 2005).

The Council for the Advancement of Standards in Higher Education (2006), a consortium of forty higher education student affairs professional organizations, has also affirmed that colleges and universities, through creation of a separate program or a unified group of programs for BGLT students, must "promote academic and personal growth and development of LGBT students, assure unrestricted access to and full involvement in all aspects of the institution, and serve as a catalyst for the creation of a campus environment free from prejudice, bigotry, harassment and violence and hospitable for all students" (p. 112).

To this end, the programs and services associated with supporting BGLT communities on campus must advocate for a campus free of violence directed at BGLT people, promote understanding of BGLT people and appreciation of queer culture, and provide adequate, trained support for BGLT students in their self-exploration. Expectations of staff members must be clearly stated and include the admonition that "staff members must strive to ensure the fair, objective, and impartial treatment of all persons with whom they deal" (Council for the Advancement of Standards in Higher Education, 2006, p. 119).

Student affairs professional socialization practices clearly demonstrate that these professionals are ethically obligated to continuously assess campus environments and practices for the ways in which such efforts support (or fail to support) the development of the BGLT student population. Graduate school is a time when those in apprenticeship for a new professional role typically become versed in that profession's values, mores, and ethics. Consciousness of responsibility for BGLT students thus logically begins with student affairs graduate preparation programs.

BGLT Issues in Professional Preparation of Student Affairs Practitioners

The inculcation of values of respect and support for BGLT persons must begin in the graduate preparation program, the point of entry for most future leaders in student affairs. Three decades of research have consistently demonstrated the importance of a maximally diverse and inclusive student body for all students' learning outcomes (Astin, 1992; Kuh and others, 2005; Pascarella and Terenzini, 2005). Thus, student affairs practitioners have both an ethical and a professional obligation to develop competency in various forms of diversity as well as learning skills and strategies for assisting students in understanding and appreciating diversity in their communities.

Given this responsibility, student affairs graduate preparation programs have a distinct role to play in supporting the competence of emerging professionals with respect to considerations of difference. The scholarship evaluating the extent to which student affairs graduate preparation programs effectively address differences has been inconclusive, however (Pope, Reynolds, and Mueller, 2004; Talbot and Kocarek, 1997). This situation may be attributable to the fact that scholars use different terminology (sometimes the operative word being measured is "diversity," other times "multiculturalism"), and they have tended to focus on the extent to which racial or ethnic and cultural differences are explicitly addressed in the curriculum (ignoring or marginalizing issues of gender identity and expression, which would be more inclusive of the specific issues of concern for transgender students).

Although the goals and objectives of incorporating expertise in diverse student identities is not yet defined consistently in the profession, most programs report that they include exposure to these concepts in their graduate preparation programs. In a survey of student affairs graduate programs conducted in 1992, 100 percent of respondents indicated that they had incorporated multicultural issues in the content, and 50 percent had required at least one course in multicultural concepts or had infused concepts of multiculturalism into several nonrequired courses (Fried, 1995). In a similar study, Flowers (2003) found that among fifty-three student affairs graduation preparation programs, three-fourths offered a required course in diversity (while acknowledging that this course may or may not include differences in sexual orientation, with no mention made of diversity of gender expression). The literature does not attest to the overall effectiveness of these courses, and some students have reported that connections between theory and practice in graduate programs, particularly where social justice issues are concerned, is weak (Kline and Gardner, 2005).

Some of the inconsistency in the quality and breadth of teaching about BGLT students in student affairs graduate programs may be attributable to faculty attitudes toward these issues. One study concluded that the comfort level of student affairs faculty with teaching about issues of women and minority students appears to be greater than teaching about BGLT issues (Talbot and Kocarek, 1997). Sanlo (2002) found that an informal Web search of titles of courses offered in graduate student affairs preparation programs across the country revealed very few that included specific reference to understanding BGLT student issues.

Scholars have called on faculty in graduate student affairs programs to begin educating themselves, and by extension their students, in the developmental theories and needs of students who are BGLT-identified (Roper, 2005; Talbot and Viento, 2005). Despite the lack of evidence for integration of BGLT issues into many or most student affairs graduate preparation programs to date, the research agendas of faculty in some graduate programs suggest that new approaches to understanding BGLT identities, including the use of post-structuralist theories (such as queer theory and feminist theory) indicates that this trend may be changing (see, for example, Abes, 2007; Abes and Kasch, 2007; Renn, 2007; Rhoads, 1997).

Conclusion

Campus resource centers for bisexual, gay, lesbian, and transgender students, founded to support them in their growth and development and to foster a sense of community among students, faculty, staff, and graduates, are diverse in their locations, foci, and resources. Ronni Sanlo noted that some are "staffed by a part-time graduate student in a tiny little space with little or no resources," and some have "two or more professional staff, a large operating budget, and a suite of offices" ("Setting Up an LGBT Center on Your Campus," 2006, p. 1). Although BGLT campus resource centers provide invaluable services for those whom they serve, the current dearth of centers at more than 90 percent of America's colleges and universities means that very few students are bene-fiting developmentally from their presence. For those who are, these centers create a sense of belonging and inclusion that is difficult to replicate in any other way or with the same impact. Students participating in BGLT campus resource centers "are seeking, among other resources, respectable headquar-ters, where they can invite professors, hold events, and develop a sense of belonging on the campus" (Lipka, 2010b).

Looking to the model of the BGLT campus resource center as exemplary for providing support and affirmation of BGLT identities, how might colleges and universities continue to offer similar forms of community building to BGLT students and, in so doing, reduce their isolation? How can colleges and universities in turn be transformed by the presence of sustained student activism in concert with intentional goals and practices? Clearly, this chapter of higher education's struggle to become socially just is only the beginning. In reflecting on the meaning of the work at one BGLT campus resource center, Zemsky (1996) said, "My hope is that we can be proud of our work in asking questions, struggling to find the answers, and continuing to seek the linkage between academics and activism" (p. 213). From the dim and shadowy past of BGLT communal life, once driven underground, students today are claim-ing a beacon, a home, in the empowerment promised by the BGLT campus resource center.

Identity and Solidarity: The Next Steps in BGLT Student Inclusion and Equity

> Students discovered that a basic commitment could overcome fears of impotence, exposure, and ridicule. Having come to "play," they stayed to defend their dignity: They demanded a different role than the image of the fumbling adolescent.
>
> —Former student activist Jerry Berman,
> quoted in Cohen and Hale, 1967, p. 240

NEARLY FORTY-TWO YEARS AFTER STONEWALL, at dusk on a Thursday evening in April 2011, an overflow crowd of eighty students, faculty, and student affairs administrators congregated in the same room where the gay student alliance once furtively met in the 1970s. The occasion was the announcement that after a ten-month process to assess the campus climate for BGLTQ students, the nation's oldest university would be opening an office of BGLTQ Student Life and hiring a full-time director to staff the office in the coming year. It was a momentous event at Harvard, not only for what it represented about the legitimacy of creating support structures for BGLTQ students there and across the country. It was equally momentous because together, three distinct groups of stakeholders—students, faculty, and student affairs administrators—brought this new initiative to life.

The forces that came together to make this particular institution amenable to this shift were formidable and diverse. Ninety years earlier, student lives and futures were upended when the then-dean and others entrusted with stewardship of the college's resources summarily routed out seven members of the community for being gay. What made it possible to transcend that shameful past and to place BGLT students and their needs squarely in the center of the conversation about the institution and its future?

Part of the explanation has to do with the degree to which concern for BGLT students' safety and ability to thrive was shared among many, rather than a few. Participants in Harvard's Working Group on BGLTQ Student Life were from many different domains of the institution's life and shape-shifted between and among them with surprising dexterity; one moment, they might be engaged in radical protest against the reinstatement of ROTC on the campus, the next, sitting in a conference room with donuts and residential life staff, pondering the ways that educational outreach to queer students and their allies could be better and more efficiently managed. What rendered this process most effective was that each member of the group contributed to the effort through her, his, or hir distinctive position. Faculty, some senior and some not, brought depth, rigor, and research sophistication to the process from their positions as scholars; student affairs administrators brought pragmatism, laced with the long view of the institution's resource priorities and politics and awareness of students' development assets and deficits. Students brought vigor, creativity, and unflinching honesty from their lived experience as talismans of their community's truth.

Stonewall happened because a group of oppressed individuals, fed up with the daily onslaught levied against them by those in power, rose up to fight back. As a singular act of resistance, Stonewall awoke the public consciousness about the rights and personhood of BGLT people, but it did not change the world overnight. Steady and sustained toil, from many different actors with many different perspectives, has shifted the course of history for BGLT people in America. Similarly, what happened at Harvard in 2010 was that a vision of BGLT advancement that hinged on sustained, thoughtful effort from the multiple and varied assets of all members of a particular college or university community enabled a broad, cross-coalition movement to form at an institution. Although radical uprisings have a vaunted place in the history of the BGLT rights movement, those with their shoulder to the wheel also create change. Reflecting on the experience of creating incremental change in concert with many others, what follows is one conceptualization of how students, faculty, and student affairs professionals can coalesce to continuously advance the agenda of BGLT inclusion and safety on their campuses through a praxis of collaborative transformation (see Figure 2).

Collaborative Transformation

Praxis, according to radical educational theorist Paulo Freire (1986), is "reflection and action upon the world in order to transform it" (p. 36). It is the application of considered, organic, and evidence-based responses to one's situation that makes transcendence plausible. Praxis can take many forms, but at its core, it is a philosophy of liberation that is inherently cyclical—that invites the breadth of our experience into the formation of strategies for change, tethering them inseparably. In the case of collaborative transformation, all experiences— perceptions, actions, and reactions—are part of the picture that is considered as stakeholders seek to address change in a unified, but not uniform, way. This approach affirms that each one seated at the table has a role to play, and, in their playing, possibilities are enlivened for genuine institutional change.

Research about the state of the strategies being used to effect change suggests that employing collaborative transformation is a logical next step in the evolution of BGLT rights movements on campus. In her analysis of the literature to date, Renn (2010) identified new directions emanating from recent scholarship on BGLT issues in higher education, including the integration of concepts from queer theory. She called for renewed attention to selection of thoughtful methods for answering questions about BGLT identities and challenges in substantive ways. While welcoming new theoretical standpoints, she also argued persuasively for maintaining commitment to education as an inherently practical endeavor, heralding the continuous fusion of assessment with creative strategies that can then be employed to address seemingly intractable problems of inequity and marginalization.

Echoing Renn's observations (2010), it is here, at the intersection of research and practice, that I wish to argue for a meaningful model of solidarity among students, faculty, and student affairs professionals in the service of queer-affirmative social change. History tells us that students have largely driven the movement for BGLT empowerment on campus. Typically embracing

FIGURE 2
Collaborative Transformation Model

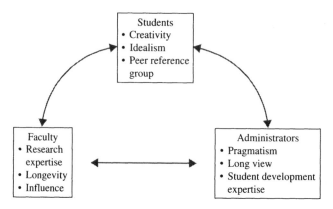

radicalism, students have claimed visibility, have organized to draw attention to their oppressions, and have challenged power structures to question (and ultimately change) their second-class status in many different institutional settings. Although student affairs administrators and faculty joined in the struggle in some instances, the momentum was largely driven by students' ingenuity and resolve. Student movements have made a tremendous difference in modification of intolerant campus environments for BGLT-identified people and have challenged the perception of students as ineffectual with their hard-won successes.

At the same time, evidence also suggests that faculty, through application of deep thinking and new constructs to the study of bisexual, gay, lesbian, and transgender lives and politics, and student affairs administrators, through carefully planned and executed assessment, patient and effective coalition building, and facility with application of student development theory to policy and practice, have also made a tremendous difference in advancing BGLT equity on campus. In ways typically less radical but no less visionary, faculty and student affairs practitioners, working as advocates and simply as concerned members of the community and its allies, have improved the climate for BGLT students at many individual institutions of higher education as well as nationally. Each performer in this play has a distinctive stance that emanates from his or her particular position, the hybrid of which can foster a network of active and engaged participation. Collaborative transformation posits that without any one of the three spokes of the wheel—rigor, pragmatism, and idealism—the result is, by definition, less robust.

That being said, students, faculty, and student affairs administrators may not come to the table as natural allies. What must be contended with to truly enact collaborative transformation? First, we must name and deconstruct our tendencies to operate in suspicion of one another's motives. Formation of community with student activists may not be a straightforward task but it is nonetheless a worthy one, and evidence suggests that it can have multiple benefits for advancement of social change. Research assessing student activists' perceptions of administrators revealed that student activists may perceive administrators as gatekeepers who relish their role in protecting the status quo, as antagonists and enemies determined to obstruct students' efforts, as (less frequently but meaningfully) supportive of their efforts, or as absentee leaders with mysterious roles and undefined levers of influence (Ropers-Huilman, Carwile, and Barnett, 2005). Given these possibilities, student activists may view administrators with skepticism, find them irrelevant, or feel further marginalized by them, but scholars have suggested that a fourth way is possible: students and student affairs administrators as collaborators (Ropers-Huilman, Carwile, and Barnett, 2005). The Working Group on BGLTQ Student Life at Harvard provides a vivid example of the potentiality inherent in meaningful alliances of student affairs administrators, faculty, and students; it reveals four specific factors that appear to characterize collaborative transformation: (1) a commitment to assessment, (2) a responsibility to the collective good, (3) recognition of each stakeholders' assets, and (4) a willingness to concede small wins for longer-term progress.

Assessment at the Center

To ensure thoughtful, focused, and substantive change, collaborative transformation makes primary the task of thoughtfully and rigorously assessing campus climate to better understand the experiences and challenges faced by BGLTQ community members in real time. The goals of collaborative transformation would be driven by careful attention to gathering data. Inviting students (and other members of the campus community) to report on their experiences with campus services and programs while living in the residence halls, interacting with peers, and taking part in curricular and cocurricular life provides compelling data about the issues and concerns these students face, which then can be used to inform plans of action. Benchmarking with national datasets, accessed through published studies and research reports, provides a barometer for the particular urgency of different concerns identified in the study; for example, the emergence of unreported hate crimes at an institution can signal renewed attention to policy development and enforcement for bias-related incidents.

Tools to conduct campus climate assessments can be used verbatim (with permission) or adapted from any number of existing rubrics available in published work and should be tailored to meet the specific needs of the campus. (For a sample campus climate assessment, see http://www.campusclimateindex .org/details/overall.aspx). Student leaders, faculty, and student affairs professionals together should confer on the nature of topics inquired about, the wording of questions, and strategies for encouraging students' participation in the assessment. Faculty and staff can marshal the necessary permissions, including (if necessary and desirable) senior administrators' endorsement and faculty buy-in to obtain endorsement by the institution's research review board. Students can amplify voice and participation by using established social and informal networks to reach out to their peers. Acknowledging that students at different points in their identity development will interface with data collection efforts in different ways, it is essential to create multiple avenues for involvement. For some, the anonymity assured by a password-protected survey will suffice; for others, an open forum replete with access to decision makers will feel like a more meaningful use of their time and input.

Responsibility to the Collective Good

Given that only 190 colleges and universities to date have a BGLT campus resource center (Consortium of Higher Education LGBT Resource Professionals, 2011), formation of a unified collaborative among student affairs administrators, faculty, and student activists is a necessity for advancement of a research-based agenda for change. Yet each member of the partnership brings distinct interests, commitments, and assets to the venture, all of which can and must be mediated in the service of the goals that can be mutually pursued. How might this collaboration most profitably happen if it is no one's job to undertake such an effort?

Student affairs professionals and faculty who identify as BGLT and their allies can initiate this collaborative by connecting with visible student leaders in BGLT student organizations. Admittedly, doing so requires a shift in thinking about one's professional responsibilities relative to one's identity. It means thinking outside the restrictive box of a job description to the moral and ethical imperatives of one's profession as they pertain to the empowerment of marginalized others. It means using one's position and power to amplify the voice of those without.

As evidenced earlier, participation in a BGLT community—coupled with recognition of students' multiple and intersecting facets of identity—is advantageous to students' development of a healthy sense of BGLT self. Ample evidence suggests that students with sustained and substantive relationship to BGLT others will thrive and that those who are socially isolated or who feel overwhelmed by the negative effects of homo-, bi-, and transphobia will not. BGLT elders and allies thus must take the onus of responsibility to initiate contact with student leaders who desire connection and community. An individual actor, or more optimally a small group of faculty and concerned student affairs professionals bridging disparate functional areas such as residential life, multicultural affairs, women's and gender studies, centers, and programs, and student activities, can coalesce with student leaders to form bonds of mentorship whose positive impact will be measured not only by goals set and achieved but also by the intangible benefit that comes from sharing seasoned and fresh perspectives in the service of solidarity.

Recognition of Each Stakeholder's Assets

Endorsing the notion of within-system change as resolutely emblematic of activism, Kezar (2010) studied student affairs administrators and faculty who partner with student activists and found that their motivations were varied and tended to shift with the nature of the agenda being pursued. The impetus for participating in change projects included past histories of involvement as student activists, involvement with community-based research projects, a commitment to developing future grassroots leaders, investment in helping marginalized groups (such as students) undertake change in an empowering way, and feeding off the energy and enthusiasm of students as a motivating force. Participants in the study felt additionally motivated by the reality that students also often brought informal power for change to the table along with access to resources not available to faculty and staff.

Faculty and administrators in Kezar's study partnered with students in three roles: as educators, mediators (of conflict between students and others), and activists-initiators. Although at times they were willing to take risks to advance change in visible ways such as participating in demonstrations, they were overall more likely to prefer working through established channels to achieve desired changes. In this way, "faculty and staff were instrumental and directly involved in mentoring students, helping them to determine strategies, helping them to negotiate with the administration, and assisting them to overcome obstacles and navigate power conditions" (Kezar, 2010, p. 471).

Collaborative transformation requires of those who engage with it absolute honesty about individual and collective constraints. Faculty and student affairs administrators cannot eschew their responsibilities to the institution that employs them, nor can they feign benign indifference to openly hostile conditions for BGLT students. They bring disciplinary expertise, a practical understanding of institutional resource constraints and priorities, and an ability to serve as liaisons between students' utopianism and the narrow foreclosure often masked by the phrase "that's how we've always done it." Students approach change with more openness, less anxiety, and more confidence—but also with less wisdom. Together, in the service of collaborative transformation, the work of forging a new reality for BGLT others at the institution simply has more staying power.

Willingness to Concede Small Wins for Longer-Term Progress

Relationship building is the cornerstone of collaborative transformation; stopping short of insisting on purely collective action, this form of praxis maintains that progress gained in a way that compromises community is not the goal. To that end, students—with their four-year institutional life cycle and sense of urgency about real-time improvement—inevitably resist the idea that changes desired right now may be less meaningful than those that a more deliberative process, keen on involving all interested parties and weighing all competing agendas, will endow. Faculty and administrators, for the sake of expediency, may wish to wave away recurring problems without considering the full range of the solution's impact. Collaborative transformation emphasizes keeping the focus on the bigger change—shifting the way the entire institution orients itself to BGLT social progress—which is by definition the more gradual one.

Window dressing, in the form of Band-Aid solutions such as the "one-off" educational speaker rather than the longer-term commitment to comprehensive safe-space education or installing more blue-light phones as opposed to tackling the more intransigent problem of the tension between and among queer students and those who harass them, feels, looks, and is markedly different from the readjustment of committing to actually eradicate the oppression of others. The hard work of assessment, analysis, goal identification, action, and further assessment precludes almost all forms of the easy win, but the payoff promised is far more rich for ending homophobia, biphobia, and transphobia on campus.

Conclusion

The mosaic formed by our increased understanding of BGLT student movements, student development paradigms, transgender student agency and inclusion, and the evolution, purposes, and strengths of BGLT campus resource centers provides a picture of how far colleges and universities have come in the four decades since a viable movement for BGLT rights became part of the landscape of these institutions in America. But reminders of the remaining work to be done abound: in the lost lives of those whose queer identities (and the hatred they inspire) overwhelm them; in the subtle but continuing marginality of transgender students and issues on campus; in the politics of inclusion that deny students at religious institutions their right to organize and be seen. We have a fairly clear idea of what helps students to feel supported and to grow safely and healthfully into BGLT identities; what is more elusive is devising a failure-proof schema for the ongoing process of institutional change.

In the four-plus decades that have passed since Stonewall, our understanding of BGLT college students, their needs and concerns, and their challenges has grown enormously. Students before Stonewall certainly experienced same-sex desire and alternative forms of gender expression and sought companionship to celebrate these identities; the consequences for doing so were sometimes empowering, and sometimes devastating. As they began to form communities in student homophile leagues and later in student organizations that gradually encompassed the full spectrum of BGLT identities, they created histories of organizing and action that moved many campuses forward in becoming places of acceptance and inclusion, particularly around allowing them to congregate for their own empowerment and to conduct outreach to the rest of the campus community. These histories of BGLT students on campus, their movements, and their activism have advanced our understanding of how campus transformation happens and the relative merits and costs of strategies students have used to employ visibility in the service of change.

Student development theories, originally developed based on insights from observing the trajectories of mostly white men as they entered adulthood from adolescence, were incomplete frames of reference for understanding the experiences of bisexual, gay, lesbian, and transgender students. Knowing what it was like to come to know one's self as BGLT changed perceptions of what normal development looks like and introduced the majority culture to the nuanced and delicate dance of negotiation of one's identity with self, family, friends, partners, and community when coming out. Recognizing that a queer identity is but one facet of becoming for students, theories that introduced the idea of intersectionality have furthered our understanding of this process. Seeing students three-dimensionally, we are better equipped to support them in navigating the at-times joyful and at-times treacherous waters of becoming authentic in a nonvalidating cultural surround.

Although each journey toward the awareness of one's self as BGLT is different, our collective understanding of how transgender students specifically emerge and thrive in campus environments is admittedly a work in progress. Sharing some aspects of coming out with their bisexual, gay, and lesbian brothers and sisters, transgender students must also contend with the specter of genderism: reflecting the default position of society at large, colleges and universities rely heavily on binary conceptions of gender to organize and regulate many aspects of student and academic life. Marshalling resiliency in the face of hostility adds an extra dimension to the self-concept transgender students must solidify during their time in college while at the same time claiming their rightful place in the larger movement for BGLT equity.

As students begin to know themselves as bisexual, gay, lesbian, and transgender, their natural impulse is to join others in community and to seek refuge and strength from the example of those who have gone before. BGLT campus resource centers, limited in number though they may be, provide a haven for students to explore and expand their vision of what is possible for their lives. Student affairs administrators leading these centers possess and practice a wide range of skills, including leadership development of students, advocacy for policy change, implementation of educational programs, and fostering intergenerational connections between students and alumni. Students who adopt these centers as their own, in tandem with the skilled tutelage of professional staff, relieve them of the need to reinvent the wheel. These centers serve as a repository of institutional memory about the way things used to be. Progress in turn becomes more robust when it has a home.

It is my contention that the challenges that remain to be addressed for full and equal participation of BGLT individuals on college and university campuses can be achieved only through this notion of collaborative transformation; otherwise, our real but isolating motivations and interests will simply render each of us alone, on islands of inaction. Instead, in community and in collaboration, the future of queer life on campus looks very bright indeed.

References

Abes, E. (2007). Applying queer theory in practice with college students: Transformation of a researcher's and participant's perspectives on identity. A case study. *Journal of LGBT Youth, 5*(1), 57–77.

Abes, E. S., and Jones, S. R. (2004). Meaning-making capacity and the dynamics of lesbian college students' multiple dimensions of identity. *Journal of College Student Development. 45*(6), 612–632.

Abes, E. S., Jones, S. R., and McEwen, M. K. (2007). Reconceptualizing the model of multiple dimensions of identity: The role of meaning-making capacity in the construction of multiple identities. *Journal of College Student Development, 48*(1), 1–22.

Abes, E. S., and Kasch, D. (2007). Using queer theory to understand lesbian college students' multiple dimensions of identity. *Journal of College Student Development, 48,* 619–636.

Adams, J. E. (1971, April 16). An expression of love—gay liberation widens the scope of human relationships. *Oberlin Review,* 6.

"Adopting a lover." (1971, May 5). *Time.* Retrieved February 11, 2011, from http://www.time .com/time/magazine/article/0,9171,943880,00.html.

"Agreement allows the ROTC to return to Harvard after decades away." (2011, March 5). *New York Times.* Retrieved March 14, 2011, from http://www.nytimes.com/2011/03/06 /education/06rotc.html?ref=education.

Albin, J. A., and Dungy, G. J. (2005). Professional associates: Journeys of colleagues in student affairs. In R. L. Sanlo (Ed.), *Gender identity and sexual orientation: Research, policy, and personal perspectives.* New Directions for Student Services, No. 111. San Francisco: Jossey-Bass.

Aldrich, R. (Ed.). (2006). *Gay life and culture: A world history.* London: Thames & Hudson Ltd.

Alexander, W. H. (2004). Homosexual and racial identity conflicts and depression among African-American gay males. *Trotter Review, 16*(1). Retrieved January 4, 2011, from http://scholarworks.umb.edu/trotter_review/vol16/iss1/8.

American College Health Association. (2010). *American College Health Association. National College Health Assessment II Reference Group Data Report, Spring 2010.* Linthicum, MD: American College Health Association.

American College Personnel Association. (2007). *Standing committee for lesbian, gay, bisexual and transgender awareness.* Retrieved November 30, 2007, from http://www.myacpa.org /sc/sclgbta/directoratemembers.cfm.

American Council on Education. (1937). The student personnel point of view. Washington, DC: American College Personnel Association. Retrieved on January 3, 2011, from http://www.myacpa.org/pub/documents/1937.pdf.

American Psychiatric Association. (1952). *Diagnostic and statistical manual of mental disorders.* Washington, DC: American Psychiatric Association.

American Psychiatric Association. (1968). *Diagnostic and statistical manual of mental disorders* (2nd ed.). Washington, DC: American Psychiatric Association.

American Psychiatric Association. (2000). *Diagnostic and statistical manual of mental disorders* (4th ed.). Washington, DC: American Psychiatric Association.

"Anti-gay comments found on dead pledge's body." (2007, January 11). *The Edge: Boston Internet Newsletter.* Retrieved April 3, 2011, from http://www.edgeboston.com/index.php? id=31037.

Arnold, K. D., and King, I. C. (1997). *College student development and academic life: Psychological, intellectual, social and moral issues.* New York: Garland.

Astin, A. W. (1992). *What matters in college? Four critical years revisited.* San Francisco: Jossey-Bass.

Bafico, S. (2006, May 1). Pride center targeted by vandals. *Daily Barometer of Oregon State University.* Retrieved January 28, 2011, from http://media.barometer.orst.edu/media/storage /paper854/news/2006/05/01/News/Pride.Center.Targeted.By.Vandals-2291974.shtml.

Batza, C. (2007). March 1971: Los Angeles gay and lesbian center is founded. In K. T. Burles (Ed.), *Great events from history: Gay, lesbian, bisexual and transgender events, 1848–2006* (pp. 222–223). Pasadena, CA: Salem Press.

Baxter Magolda, M. B. (2001). *Making their own way: Narratives for transforming higher education to promote self-development.* Sterling, VA: Stylus.

Bayer, R. B. (1981). *Homosexuality and American society.* New York: Basic Books.

Beemyn, B. (2002). The development and administration of campus LGBT centers and offices. In R. L. Sanlo, S. R. Rankin, and R. Schoenberg (Eds.), *Our place on campus: Lesbian, gay, bisexual, transgender services and programs in higher education* (pp. 25–40). Westport, CT: Greenwood Press.

Beemyn, B. (2003a). Serving the needs of transgender college students. *Journal of Gay and Lesbian Issues in Education, 3*(1), 33–49.

Beemyn, B. (2003b). The silence is broken: A history of the first lesbian, gay, and bisexual student groups. *Journal of the History of Sexuality, 12*(2), 205–223.

Beemyn, B. (2005). Making campuses more inclusive of transgender students. *Journal of Gay and Lesbian Issues in Education, 3*(1), 77–88.

Beemyn, B. G. and Rankin, S. (forthcoming). *The lives of transgender people.* New York: Columbia University Press.

Beemyn, B., Curtis, B., Davis, M., and Tubbs, N. J. (2005). Transgender issues on college campuses. In R. L. Sanlo (Ed.), *Gender identity and sexual orientation: Research, policy, and personal perspectives.* New Directions for Studet Services, No. 111. San Francisco: Jossey-Bass.

Beemyn, B., Domingue, A., Pettitt, J., and Smith, T. (2005). Suggested steps to make campuses more trans-inclusive. *Journal of Gay and Lesbian Issues in Education, 3*(1), 89–95.

Beemyn, G. (2007, Feb.). The lives of transgender people in the 21st century. Presentation at the Translating Identity Conference, Burlington, Vermont. Retrieved January 4, 2011, from http://www.umass.edu/stonewall/uploads/listWidget/11925/tic.pdf.

Belenky, M. F., Clinchy, B. M., Goldberger, N. R., and Tarule, J. M. (1986). *Women's Ways of Knowing.* New York: Basic Books.

Beren, S. E., Hayden, H. A., Wilfley, D. E., and Striegel-Moore, R. H. (1997). Body dissatisfaction among lesbian college students: The conflict of straddling mainstream and lesbian cultures. *Psychology of Women Quarterly, 21,* 431–445.

Bieschke, K. J., Eberz, A. B., and Wilson, D. (2000). Empirical investigations of the gay, lesbian, and bisexual college student. In V. A. Wall and N. J. Evans (Eds.), *Toward acceptance: Sexual orientation issues on campus* (pp. 29–58). Lanham, MD: University Press of America.

Bilodeau, B. (2005a). Beyond the gender binary: A case study of two transgender students at a midwestern research university. *Journal of Gay and Lesbian Issues in Education, 3*(1), 29–44.

Bilodeau, B. (2005b, Nov.). *Genderism: Binary gender systems at two midwestern universities.* Paper presented at an annual meeting of the Association for the Study of Higher Education, Philadelphia, PA.

Bilodeau, B. (2007). Genderism: Transgender students, binary systems, and higher education. *Dissertation Abstracts International, 68*(05). Proquest Document ID 134279351.

Bilodeau, B., and Renn, K. (2005). Analysis of LGBT identity development models and implications for practice. In B. L. Sanlo (Ed.), *Gender identity and sexual orientation: Research, policy, and personal perspectives.* New Directions for Student Services, No. 111. San Francisco: Jossey-Bass.

Blake, N. (2006, May 17). "Queer agenda" revisited. *Daily Barometer of Oregon State University.* Retrieved February 4, 2011, from http://media.barometer.orst.edu/media/storage/paper854/news/2006/05/17/Forum/queer.Agenda.Revisited-2291807.shtml.

Bornstein, K. (1994). *Gender outlaws: Men, women, and the rest of us.* New York: Routledge.

Borrego, A. M. (2001, Dec. 21). Today's students want to have sex, but not with their roommates. *Chronicle of Higher Education,* A29.

Bostwick, W. B., and others. (2007). Drinking patterns, problems, and motivations among collegiate bisexual women. *Journal of American College Health, 56*(3), 285–292.

"Boycott Morrie's." (1970, Dec. 4). *Cornell Daily Sun, 87*(53), 4.

Boyer, E. (1990). *Campus life: In search of community.* Princeton, NJ: The Foundation.

Boykin, K. (1996). *One more river to cross: Black and gay in America.* New York: Anchor.

Bradley, D. J. (2007). Subcutaneous: The life experience of African American transsexual college students. *Dissertation Abstracts International, 68*(08), UMI 3279174.

Brenner, B. (1972, April 20). An invisible minority: Gay Cornellians. *Cornell Daily Sun, 87*(129), 7.

Brown, R. D., Clarke, B., Gortmaker, V., and Robinson-Keilig, R. (2004). Assessing the campus climate for gay, lesbian, bisexual and transgender students using a multiple perspectives approach. *Journal of College Student Development, 45*(1), 8–26.

Browning, C., and Walsh, P. (2002). LGBT peer counselors. In R. L. Sanlo, S. R. Rankin, and R. Schoenberg (Eds.), *Our place on campus: Lesbian, gay, bisexual, transgender services and programs in higher education* (pp. 150–157). Westport, CT: Greenwood Press.

Brune, A. (2007, April 8). When she graduates as he. *Boston Globe Magazine,* 28–33.

"Building a GLBT center from the ground up." (2005, May 1). *Student Affairs Leader, 33*(9), 1–2.

Bullough, V. (2002). *Before Stonewall; Activists for gay and lesbian rights in historical context.* New York: Harrington Park Press.

Burgess, C. (1999). Internal and external stress factors associated with identity development of transgendered youth. In G. Mallon (Ed.), *Social services with transgendered youth* (pp. 35–47). New York: Harrington Park Press.

Butler, J. (1990). *Gender trouble: Feminism and the subversion of identity.* New York: Routledge.

Calhoun, P. (1974, March 13). Homosexuality shrouded in mystery. *Cornell Daily Sun, 100*(104), 6.

Califia, P. (1997). *Sex changes: The politics of transgenderism.* San Francisco: Cleis Press.

Campus Pride. (2011). LGBT-friendly campus climate index. Charlotte, NC: Campus Pride. Retrieved February 6, 2011, from http://www.CampusClimateIndex.org/.

Carson, K. (2007). 1897: Ellis publishes sexual inversion. In K. T. Burles (Ed.), *Great events from history: Gay, lesbian, bisexual and transgender events, 1848–2006* (pp. 33–35). Pasadena, CA: Salem Press.

Carter, D. (2004). *Stonewall: The riots that sparked the gay revolution.* New York: St. Martin's Press.

Carter, K. A. (2000). Transgenderism and college students: Issues of gender identity and its role on our campuses. In V. A. Wall and N. J. Evans (Eds.), *Toward acceptance: Sexual orientation issues on campus.* (pp. 261–282). Lanham, MD: University Press of America.

Cass, V. C. (1984). Homosexual identity formation: Testing a theoretical model. *Journal of Sex Research, 20*(2), 143–167.

Center for Collegiate Mental Health. (2010). *2010 Annual report.* Retrieved January 3, 2011, from http://ccmh.squarespace.com/storage/CCMH_2010_Annual_Report.pdf.

Chauncey, G. (1994). *Gay New York: Gender, urban culture, and the making of the gay male world, 1890–1940.* New York: Basic Books.

Chess, S., Kafer, A., Quizar, J., and Richardson, M. R. (2004). Calling all restroom revolutionaries! In M. B. Sycamore (Ed.), *That's revolting: Queer strategies for resisting assimilation* (pp. 216–236). Brooklyn, NY: Soft Skull Press.

Chickering, A. W. (1969). *Education and identity.* San Francisco: Jossey-Bass.

Chickering, A. W., and Reisser, L. (1993). *Education and identity* (2nd ed.). San Francisco: Jossey-Bass.

Christian, T. Y. (2005). "Good cake": An ethnographic trilogy of life satisfaction among gay black men. *Men and Masculinities, 8*(2), 164–174.

Chronicle of Higher Education Almanac. (2010, Aug. 22). Attitudes and characteristics of freshmen at four-year colleges, 2009. Retrieved February 1, 2011, from http://chronicle.com/article/AttitudesCharacteristics/124000/.

Cintron, R. (2000). Ethnicity, race, and culture: The case of Latino gay/bisexual men. In V. A. Wall and N. J. Evans (Eds.), *Toward acceptance: Sexual orientation issues on campus* (pp. 299–320). Lanham, MD: University Press of America.

Clark, C. (2005). Diversity initiatives in higher education: Deconstructing "the down low"—people of color "comin' out" and "being out" on campus. A conversation with Mark Brimhall-Vargas, Sivagami Subbaraman, and Robert Waters. *Multicultural Education, 13*(1), 45–59.

Clendinen, D., and Nagourney, A. (1999). *Out for good: The struggle to build a gay rights movement in America.* New York: Simon & Schuster.

Cohen, M., and Hale, D. (Eds.) (1967). *The new student left: An anthology.* Boston: Beacon.

Collins, P. H. (2000). Gender, black feminism, and black political economy. *Annals of the American Academy of Political and Social Science, 568,* 41–53.

Consortium of Higher Education LGBT Resource Professionals. (2011). Retrieved January 21, 2011, from http://www.lgbtcampus.org/directory/index.php?pageno=9.

Conway, L. (2002). How frequently does transsexualism occur? Retrieved February 4, 2011, from ai.eecs.umich.edu/people/conway/TS/TSprevalence.html.

Cornell University Lesbian, Gay, Bisexual and Transgender Resource Center. (2011). Retrieved February 2, 2011, from http://lgbtrc.cornell.edu/.

Council for the Advancement of Standards in Higher Education. (2006). *CAS professional standards for higher education* (6th ed.). Washington, DC: Council for the Advancement of Standards in Higher Education.

Courvant, D., and Cook-Daniels, L. (1998). Transgender and intersex survivors of domestic violence: Defining terms, barriers and responsibilities. In *National Coalition Against Domestic Violence Conference Manual* (POB 18749). Denver: National Coalition Against Domestic Violence.

Crenshaw, K. (1991). Mapping the margins: Intersectionality, identity politics, and violence against women of color. *Stanford Law Review, 43,* 1241–1279.

Cross, W. E. (1971). The Thomas and Cross models of psychological nigrescence: A review. *Journal of Black Psychology, 5,* 13–31.

Croteau, J. M., and Lark, J. S. (1995). A qualitative investigation of blased and exemplary student affairs practice concerning lesbian, gay and bisexual issues. *Journal of College Student Development, 36,* 472–482.

D'Augelli, A. R. (1989). Lesbians and gay men on campus: Visibility, empowerment, and educational leadership. *Peabody Journal of Education, 66*(3), 124–142.

D'Augelli, A. R. (1994a). Identity development and sexual orientation: Toward a model of lesbian, gay, and bisexual identity development. In E. J. Trickett, R. J. Watts, and D. Birman (Eds.), *Human diversity: Perspectives on people in context* (pp. 312–333). San Francisco: Jossey-Bass.

D'Augelli, A. R. (1994b). Lesbian and gay male development: Steps toward an analysis of lesbians' and gay men's lives. In B. Greene and G. M. Herek (Eds.), *Lesbian and gay psychology: Theory, research, and clinical applications* (pp. 118–132). Newbury Park, CA: Sage.

Dazio, S. (2011, January 10). AU readies for Westboro Baptist Church protest. *American University Eagle Online*. Retrieved February 3, 2011, from http://www.theeagleonline.com/news/story/westboro-baptist-church-to-protest-at-au-jan.-14/.

D'Emilio, J. (1992). *Making trouble: Essays on gay history, politics, and the university.* New York: Routledge.

Denizet-Lewis, B. (2010, June 1). The secret court. *The Good Men Project Magazine.* Retrieved December 4, 2010, from http://goodmenproject.com/featured-content/the-secret-court/.

Devor, A. H. (2004). Witnessing and mirroring: A fourteen-stage model of transsexual identity formation. *Journal of Gay and Lesbian Psychotherapy, 8*(1/2), 41–67.

Diamond, L. M. (2000). Sexual identity, attractions, and behavior among young sexual-minority women over a 2-year period. *Developmental Psychology, 36*(2), 241–250.

Diamond, L. M. (2005). What we got wrong about sexual identity development: Unexpected findings from a longitudinal study of young women. In A. Omoto and H. Kurtzman (Eds.), *Sexual orientation and mental health: Examining identity and development in lesbian, gay, and bisexual people* (pp. 73–94). Washington, DC: American Psychological Association Press.

Diaz, E. M., and Kosciw, J. G. (2009). *Shared differences: The experiences of lesbian, gay, bisexual and transgender students of color in our nation's schools.* New York: Gay, Lesbian, Straight Educators Network.

Dilley, P. (2002a*). Queer man on campus: A history of non-heterosexual college men, 1945–2000.* New York: Routledge Falmer.

Dilley, P. (2002b). 20th century postsecondary practices and policies to control gay students. *Review of Higher Education, 25*(4), 409–431.

Dilley, P. (2004). LGBTQ research in higher education: A review of articles, 2000–2003. *Journal of Gay and Lesbian Issues in Education, 2*(2), 105–115.

Dilley, P. (2010). New century, new identities: Building on a typology of nonheterosexual college men. *Journal of LGBT Youth, 7*(3), 186–199.

DiPerna, J. (2006, Aug. 17). Penn State's Portland in a storm. *Pittsburgh City Paper.* Retrieved June 28, 2011, from http://www.pittsburghcitypaper.ws/gyrobase/Content? oid=oid:19317.

Donaldson, S. (1992). Student homophile league: Founder's retrospect. In W. R. Dynes (Ed.), *Homosexuality and government, politics, and prisons* (pp. 258–261). New York: Garland.

Dube, E. M., and Savin-Williams, R. C. (1999). Sexual identity development among ethnic sexual minority male youths. *Developmental Psychology, 35*(6), 1389–1398.

Duberman, M. (1993). *Stonewall.* New York: Penguin Books.

Dumas, M. J. (1998). Coming out/coming home: Black gay men on campus. In R. Sanlo, (Ed.), *Working with lesbian, gay, bisexual and transgender college students: A handbook for administrators* (pp. 79–85). Westport, CT: Greenwood Press.

Dynes, W. R. (1990). *Encyclopedia of homosexuality.* New York: Garland.

Dynes, W. R. (2002). Stephen Donaldson (Robert Martin), 1946–1996. In V. Bullough (Ed.), *Before Stonewall: Activists for gay and lesbian rights in historical context* (pp. 265–272). New York: Harrington Park Press.

Eckholm, E. (2011, April 18). Gay rights at Christian colleges face suppression. *New York Times*. Retrieved April 23, 2011, from http://www.nytimes.com/2011/04/19/us /19gays.html?_r=2andhp.

Ecksmith, L. (1971, March 19). Students consider organizing gay lib. *Oberlin Review*. Retrieved January 3, 2011, from http://www.oberlinlgbt.org/content/Historical -Documents/The-1970s/students-consider-organizing-gay-lib.html.

Eddy, W., and Forney, D. S. (2000). Assessing campus environments for the lesbian, gay, and bisexual population. In V. A. Wall and N. J. Evans (Eds.), *Toward acceptance: Sexual orientation issues on campus* (pp. 131–154). Lanham, MD: University Press of America.

Edsall, N. C. (2003). *Toward Stonewall: Homosexuality and society in the modern western world*. Charlottesville: University of Virginia.

Eisenberg, M. E., and Wechsler, H. (2003). Social influences on substance-use behaviors of gay, lesbian, and bisexual college students: Findings from a national study. *Social Science and Medicine, 57*, 1913–1923.

Eliason, M. (1996). Identity formation for lesbian, gay, and bisexual persons: Beyond a minoritizing view. *Journal of Homosexuality, 30*(3), 31–58.

Estrada, D., and Rutter, P. (2006). Using the multiple lenses of identity: Working with ethnic and sexual minority college students. *Journal of College Counseling, 9*(2), 158–166.

Evans, N. J. (2001). The experiences of lesbian and gay youths in university communities. In A. R. D'Augelli and C. J. Patterson (Eds.), *Lesbian, gay, and bisexual identities and youth: Psychological perspectives* (pp. 181–198). New York: Oxford University Press.

Evans, N. J., and Broido, E. M. (1999). Coming out in college residence halls: Meaning making, challenges, and supports. *Journal of College Student Development, 40*, 658–668.

Evans, N. J., and others. (2010). *Student development in college: Theory, research and practice* (2nd ed.). San Francisco: Jossey-Bass.

Evans, N. J., and Wall, V. A. (1991). *Beyond tolerance: Gays, lesbians and bisexuals on campus*. Lanham, MD: University Press of America.

Eyermann, T., and Sanlo, R. L. (2002). Documenting their existence: Lesbian, gay, bisexual, and transgender students on campus. In R. L. Sanlo, S. R. Rankin, and R. Schoenberg (Eds.), *Our place on campus: Lesbian, gay, bisexual, transgender services and programs in higher education* (pp. 33–40). Westport, CT: Greenwood Press.

Faderman, L. (1991). *Odd girls and twilight lovers: A history of lesbian life in America*. New York: Columbia University Press.

Faderman, L. (1999). *To believe in women: What lesbians have done for America. A history*. Boston: Houghton Mifflin.

Fassinger, R. E. (1998). Lesbian, gay and bisexual identity and student development theory. In R. L. Sanlo (Ed.), *Working with lesbian, gay, bisexual and transgender college students: A handbook for faculty and administrators* (pp. 13–22). Westport, CT: Greenwood Press.

Federal Bureau of Investigation. (2011). Hate crime statistics, 2006. Retrieved February 3, 2011, from http://www.fbi.gov/about-us/cjis/ucr/hate-crime/2006.

Feinberg, L. (1996). *Transgender warriors: Making history from Joan of Arc to RuPaul*. Boston: Beacon Press.

Ferguson, A. D., and Howard-Hamilton, M. F. (2000). Addressing issues of multiple identities for women of color on college campuses. In V. A. Wall and N. J. Evans (Eds.), *Toward acceptance: Sexual orientation issues on campus* (pp. 283–299). Lanham, MD: University Press of America.

Fisher, B. S., Cullen, F. T., and Turner, M. G. (2000). *The sexual victimization of college women.* Washington, DC: U.S. Department of Justice, Office of Justice Programs.

Fishman, L. (2010, April 30). Student attacked at CSU–Long Beach in transgender hate crime. *Los Angeles Criminal Law Blog.* Retrieved March 3, 2011, from http://www.ktla .com/news/landing/ktla-csulb-student-slashed,0,5414609.story.

Flowers, L. (2000). *Diversity issues in American colleges and universities: Case studies for higher education and student affairs professionals.* Springfield, IL: Charles C. Thomas Publishers.

Flowers, L. (2003). National study of diversity requirements in student affairs graduate programs. *NASPA journal, 40*(4), 72–82.

Foderaro, L. (2010, September 29). Private moment made public, then a fatal jump. *New York Times.* Retrieved November 24, 2010, from http://www.nytimes.com/2010/09/30 /nyregion/30suicide.html.

Foster, T. A. (Ed.). (2007). *Long before Stonewall: Histories of same-sex sexuality in early America.* New York: New York University Press.

Freire, P. (1986). *Pedagogy of the oppressed* (2nd ed.). New York: Continuum.

French, L. (2009, Feb. 23). Ousted ROTC student praised: Student's saga spurs protest of "don't ask." *The Hatchet of George Washington University.* Retrieved February 3, 2011, from http://media.www.gwhatchet.com/media/storage/paper332/news/2009/02/23 /News/Ousted.Rotc.Student.Praised-3643205.shtml.

Fried, I. (2000). It's a long journey, so bring an extra set of clothes. In K. Howard and A. Stevens (Eds.), *Out and about on campus: Personal accounts by lesbian, gay, bisexual and transgendered college students* (pp. 244–255). Los Angeles: Alyson Books.

Fried, J. (1995). *Shifting paradigms in student affairs: Culture, context, teaching and learning.* Lanham, MD: University Press of America.

Friedan, B. (1963). *The feminine mystique.* New York: Norton & Co.

Friess, S. (2007, April 30). Do ask, do tell at BYU. *Newsweek, 149*(18). Retrieved January 4, 2011, from http://www.newsweek.com/2007/04/29/do-ask-do-tell-at-byu.html.

Frye, P. F. (2000). Facing discrimination, organizing for freedom: The transgender community. In J. D'Emilio, W. B. Turner, and U. Vaid (Eds.), *Creating change: Sexuality, public policy, and civil rights* (pp. 451–468). New York: St. Martin's Press.

Fukuyama, M. A., and Ferguson, A. D. (2000). Lesbian, gay, and bisexual people of color: Understanding cultural complexity and managing multiple oppressions. In R. M. Perez, K. A. DeBord, and K. J. Bieshke (Eds.), *Handbook of counseling and psychotherapy with lesbian, gay, and bisexual clients* (pp. 81–106). Washington, DC: American Psychological Association.

Gallagher, A. (2011, March 28). Second pride parade nearly doubles in size. *Daily Collegian of Penn State University.* Retrieved April 2, 2011, from http://www.collegian.psu.edu /archive/2011/03/28/pride_week_parade.aspx.

Gallo, M. (2006). *Different daughters: A history of the Daughters of Bilitis and the lesbian rights movement.* New York: Carroll & Graf.

Gallo, M. (2007). 1955: Daughters of Bilitis founded as first national lesbian group in United States. In K. T. Burles (Ed.), *Great events from history: Gay, lesbian, bisexual and transgender events, 1848–2006* (pp. 132–134). Pasadena, CA: Salem Press.

Gan, J. (2007). Still at the back of the bus: Sylvia Rivera's struggle. *Centro Journal, 19*(1), 124–139.

Garnets, L. D., and Kimmel, D. C. (1993). *Psychological perspectives on lesbians and gay male experiences.* New York: Columbia University Press.

Gilligan, C. (1982). *In a different voice.* Cambridge, MA: Harvard University Press.

Gortmaker, V. J., and Brown, R. D. (2006). Out of the college closet: Differences in perceptions and experiences among out and closeted lesbian and gay students. *College Student Journal, 40*(3), 606–619.

Grant, J. M., and others. (2011). *Injustice at every turn: A report of the National Transgender Discrimination Survey.* Washington, DC: National Center for Transgender Equality and National Gay and Lesbian Task Force.

Gray, A. (2000). Wearing the dress. In K. Howard and A. Stevens (Eds.) *Out and about on campus: Personal accounts by lesbian, gay, bisexual and transgendered college students* (pp. 83–92). Los Angeles: Alyson Books.

Greenaway, E. T. (2001, June 12). Girls will be boys. *Alternet.* Retrieved January 28, 2011, from http://www.alternet.org/story/11017/.

Griffin, P., and Carroll, H. J. (2010, October 4). *On the team: Equal opportunity for transgender student athletes.* National Center for Lesbian Rights. Retrieved April 26, 2011, from http://www.nclrights.org/site/DocServer/TransgenderStudentAthleteReport.pdf?docID =7901.

Halpin, S. A., and Allen, M. W. (2004). Changes in psychosocial well-being during gay identity development. *Journal of homosexuality, 47*(2), 109–126.

Hanson, D. E. (2010, Nov. 10). Institutions can launch assessments of their LGBT climate, but should they? *NetResults: Critical Issues for Student Affairs Practitioners.* National Association of Student Personnel Administrators. Retrieved December 4, 2010, from http://www.naspa.org/membership/mem/pubs/nr/default.cfm?id=1756.

Harding University Queer Press. (2011). *The state of the gay at Harding University.* Retrieved March 2, 2011, from http://huqueerpress.com/the_zine.html.

Harley, D. A., Nowak, T. A., Gassaway, L. J., and Savage, T. A. (2002). Lesbian, gay, bisexual, and transgender college students with disabilities: A look at multiple cultural minorities. *Psychology in the Schools, 39*(5), 525–538.

Harper, S. R. (2004). The measure of a man: Conceptualizations of masculinity among high-achieving African American male college students. *Berkeley Journal of Sociology, 48*(1), 89–107.

Harris, F., III. (2008). Deconstructing masculinity: A qualitative study of college men's masculine conceptualizations and gender performance. *NASPA Journal, 45*(4), 453–474.

Harris, W. G. (2003). African American homosexual males on predominantly white college and university campuses. *Journal of African American Studies, 7*(1), 47–56.

"Harvard ends four-decade ban on ROTC, Yale next." (2011, March 5). *New Haven Register.* Retrieved March 16, 2011, from http://www.nhregister.com/articles/2011/03/05/news/aa9harvardrotc5030411.txt.

Helms, J. E. (Ed.). (1990). *Black and white racial identity: Theory, research and practice.* Westport, CT: Greenwood Press.

Henning-Stout, M., James, S., and Macintosh, S. (2000). Reducing harassment of lesbian, gay, bisexual, transgender, and questioning youth in schools. *School Psychology Review, 29*(2), 180–191.

Henry, W. J., Fuerth, K., and Figliozzi, J. (2010). Gay with a disability: A college student's multiple cultural journey. *College Student Journal, 44*(2), 377–388.

Herbenick, D., and others. (2010). Sexual behavior in the United States: Results from a national probability survey of men and women age 14–94. *Journal of Sexual Medicine, 7*(5), 255–266.

Highleyman, L. (2007a). April 19, 1967: First student homophile league is formed. In K. T. Burles (Ed.), *Great events from history: Gay, lesbian, bisexual and transgender events, 1848–2006* (pp. 172–175). Pasadena, CA: Salem Press.

Highleyman, L. (2007b). August 1966: Queer youth fight police harassment at Compton's cafeteria in San Francisco. In K. T. Burles (Ed.), *Great events from history: Gay, lesbian, bisexual and transgender events, 1848–2006* (pp. 163–165). Pasadena, CA: Salem Press.

Hill, D., and Willoughby, B. (2005). Development and validation of the genderism and transphobia scale. *Sex roles, 53,* 531–544.

History Project. (1998). *Improper Bostonians: Lesbian and gay history from the Puritans to Playland.* Boston: Beacon Press.

Holleran, A. (1997). My Harvard. In R. Schneider Jr. (Ed.), *The best of* The Harvard Gay and Lesbian Review (pp. 4–19). Philadelphia: Temple University Press.

Hooker, E. (1961). Homosexuality: Summary of studies. In E. M. Duvall and S. Duvall (Eds.), *Sex ways in fact and faith: Bases for Christian family policy.* New York: Association Press.

Hoover, E. (2006, April 28). Gay and Christian: A student suspended from a Baptist university adjusts to his role in the national spotlight. *Chronicle of Higher Education, 52*(34), A46.

Horowitz, H. L. (1984). *Alma Mater: Design and experience in the women's colleges from their nineteenth-century beginnings to the 1930s.* New York: Knopf.

Howard, K., and Stevens, A. (2000). *Out and about on campus: Personal accounts by lesbian, gay, bisexual and transgender college students.* Los Angeles: Alyson Books.

Human Rights Campaign. (n.d.). Transgender Americans: A handbook for understanding. Retrieved February 3, 2011, from http://www.hrc.org/documents/Transgender_hand book.pdf.

Hunter, S. (2007a). 1950: Mattachine society is founded. In K. T. Burles (Ed.), *Great events from history: Gay, lesbian, bisexual and transgender events, 1848–2006* (pp. 106–107). Pasadena, CA: Salem Press.

Hunter, S. (2007b). 1994: National Association of Lesbian and Gay Community centers is founded. In K. T. Burles (Ed.), *Great events from history: Gay, lesbian, bisexual and transgender events, 1848–2006* (pp. 621–623). Pasadena, CA: Salem Press.

Icard, L. D. (1996). Assessing the psychosocial well-being of African American gays: A multidimensional perspective. *Journal of Gay and Lesbian Social Services, 5*(2/3), 25–38.

Inness, S. A. (1994). Mashes, smashes, crushes and raves: Woman-to-woman relationships in popular women's college fiction, 1895–1915. *NWSA Journal, 6*(1), 48–68.

Institute for Sex Research. (1953). *Sexual behavior in the human female.* Philadelphia: W. B. Saunders Co.

Ivory, B. T. (2005). LGBT students in community colleges: Characteristics, challenges, and recommendations. In R. L. Sanlo (Ed.), *Gender identity and sexual orientation: Research, policy, and personal perspectives.* New Directions for Student Services, No. 111. San Francisco: Jossey-Bass.

Jay, K. (1999). *Tales of the lavender menace: A memoir of liberation.* New York: Basic Books.

Jones, S. R., and McEwen, M. K. (2000). A conceptual model of multiple dimensions of identity. *Journal of College Student Development, 41*(4), 405–414.

Kardia, D. (2007). July 31, 1969: Gay liberation front is founded. In K. T. Burles (Ed.), *Great events from history: Gay, lesbian, bisexual and transgender events, 1848–2006* (pp. 195–198). Pasadena, CA: Salem Press.

Katz, J. N. (1992). *Gay American history: Lesbians and gay men in the U.S.A.* (Rev. ed.). New York: Penguin Books.

Kauffman, J. M., and Johnson, C. (2004). Stigmatized individuals and the process of identity. *Sociological Quarterly, 45*(4), 807–833.

Kellogg, A. P. (2001, March 30). Brigham Young U. suspends one gay student, forces another to drop out. *Chronicle of Higher Education.* Retrieved January 1, 2011, from http://chronicle.com/article/Brigham-Young-U-Suspends-One/107497/.

Kellogg, A. P. (2002, Jan. 18). "Safe sex fatigue" grows among gay students. *Chronicle of Higher Education, 48*(19), A37.

Kezar, A. (2010). Faculty and staff partnering with student activists: Unexplored terrains of action and development. *Journal of College Student Development, 51*(5), 451–480.

Kinsey, A. (1948). *Sexual behavior in the human male.* Philadelphia: W. B. Saunders.

Kline, K. A., and Gardner, M. M. (2005). Envisioning new forms of praxis: Reflective practice and social justice education in higher education graduate programs. *Advancing Women in Leadership, 191*, 5–11.

Kohlberg, L. (1971). Stages of moral development. In C. M. Beck, B. S. Crittenden, and E. V. Sullivan (Eds.), *Moral education.* Toronto: University of Toronto Press.

Kosciw, J., and Diaz, E. M. (2006). *The 2005 National School Climate Survey: The experiences of lesbian, gay, bisexual and transgender youth in our schools.* New York: Gay, Lesbian, Straight Educators Network (GLSEN).

Kosciw, J. G., Greytak, E. A., Diaz, E. M., and Bartkiewicz, M. J. (2010). *The 2009 National School Climate Survey: The experiences of lesbian, gay, bisexual and transgender youth in our nation's schools.* New York: GLSEN.

Kuh, G., and others. (2005). *Student success in college: Creating conditions that matter*. San Francisco: Jossey-Bass.

Kulick, D. (2000). Gay and lesbian language. *Annual Review of Anthropology, 29*, 243–285.

Lauritsen, J. (1998). *Queer nation*. Retrieved March 2, 2011, from http://paganpressbooks.com/jpl/Q-JL.HTM.

Lees, L. J. (1998). Transgender students on our campuses. In R. L. Sanlo (Ed.), *Working with lesbian, gay, bisexual, and transgender college students: A handbook for faculty and administrators* (pp. 37–47). Westport, CT: Greenwood Educators Reference Collection.

Levine, H., and Love, P. G. (2000). Religiously affiliated institutions and sexual orientation. In V. A. Wall and N. J. Evans (Eds.), *Toward acceptance: Sexual orientation issues on campus* (pp. 89–108). Lanham, MD: University Press of America.

Lewis, C. H. (2010). *Prescription for heterosexuality: Sexual citizenship in the cold war era*. Chapel Hill: University of North Carolina Press.

Lipka, S. (2010a, March 16). Approval of gay marriage is greater among college freshmen than Americans at large. *Chronicle of Higher Education*. Retrieved January 2, 2011, from http://chronicle.com/article/College-Freshmen-Approve-of/64685/.

Lipka, S. (2010b, March 6). For gay students, more room on campuses. *Chronicle of Higher Education*. Retrieved March 15, 2011, from http://chronicle.com/article/For-Gay-Students-More-Room-on/126608/.

Loffreda, B. (2001). *Losing Matt Shepard: Life and politics in the aftermath of an anti-gay murder*. New York: Columbia University Press.

Loiacano, D. K. (1989). Gay identity issues among black Americans: Racism, homophobia, and the need for validation. *Journal of Counseling and Development, 68*(1), 21–25.

Lynch, B. (2010). Affirmation of transgender students: Evaluation of a rural New England college. *Dissertation Abstracts International*, 71(07), UMI 3415601.

MacKay, A. (Ed.). (1993). *Wolf girls at Vassar: Lesbian and gay experiences*. New York: St. Martin's Press.

Mallon, G. P. (1999). *Social services with transgender youth*. New York: Harrington Park Press.

Marine, S. B. (2009). Navigating discourses of discomfort: Women's college student affairs administrators and transgender students. *Dissertation Abstracts International*, 70(02), UMI 3349517.

Marklein, M. (2004, June 21). Gender neutral comes to campus. *USA Today, 9*.

McCauley, C. (1985, March 25). GSS to provide support for homosexual students. *Penn State Daily Collegian, 5*.

McCray, P., and Marston, B. (1991). *Guide to the Cornell Lesbian, Gay, Bisexual, and Transgender Coalition records, 1968–1999*. Division of rare and manuscript collections, Cornell University Library. Retrieved February 4, 2011, from http://rmc.library.cornell.edu/EAD/htmldocs/RMA01589.html.

McKee, M. (2010, November 29). Westboro Baptist Church says it's heading to Brandeis, Wayland, and Framingham Friday. *Boston.com web news source*. Retrieved January 4, 2011, from http://www.boston.com/yourtown/news/waltham/2010/11/westboro_baptist_church_says_i.html.

McKinney, J. S. (2005). On the margins: A study of the experiences of transgender college students. *Journal of Gay and Lesbian Issues in Education, 3*(1), 63–77.

Mitchell, S. A. (1978). Psychodynamics, homosexuality, and the question of pathology. *Psychiatry: Journal for the Study of Interpersonal Processes, 41*(3), 254–263.

Money, J. (1994). The concept of gender identity disorder in childhood and adolescence after 39 years. *Journal of Sex and Marital Therapy, 20*(3), 163–177.

Mooney, C. (1994, Nov. 16). Religion vs. gay rights: Teshiva U. debates whether recognition of gay groups threatens its identity. *Chronicle of Higher Education.* Retrieved January 13, 2011, from http://chronicle.com/article/Religion-vs-Gay-Rights/85236/.

Morais, B., and Schreiber, L. (2007, December 7). Transgender students search for campus niche. *Columbia Spectator.* Retrieved January 2, 2008, from www.columbiaspectator.com /?q=node/28536.

Morgan, R. (2002, Nov. 29). Bisexual students face tension with gay groups. *Chronicle of Higher Education, 49*(14), A31.

Morgan, S. W., and Stevens, P. E. (2008). Transgender identity development as represented by a group of female-to-male transgendered adults. *Issues in Mental Health Nursing, 29,* 585–599.

Morrison, T. (1987). *Beloved.* New York: Knopf.

Moser, J. (2004, May 28). Queer resource center to be renamed, will move to new location. *Oregon State University Daily Barometer.* Retrieved February 2, 2011, from http://media .barometer.orst.edu/media/storage/paper854/news/2004/05/28/News/Qrc-Asks.Whats .In.A.Name-2299755.shtml.

Nakamura, K. (1998). Transitioning on campus: A case studies approach. In R. L. Sanlo (Ed.), *Working with lesbian, gay, bisexual, and transgender college students: A handbook for faculty and administrators* (pp. 179–187). Westport, CT: Greenwood Educators Reference Collection.

Namaste, V. K. (2000). *Invisible lives: The erasure of transsexual and transgendered people.* Chicago: University of Chicago Press.

National Association of Student Personnel Administrators. (2007*). Lesbian, gay, bisexual and transgender issues knowledge community description.* Retrieved December 9, 2010, from http://www.naspa.org/communities/kc/community.cfm?kcid=7.

National Association of Student Personnel Administrators. (2010). *Voices out loud: National convention newsletter of the GLBT concerns knowledge community.* Retrieved March 19, 2011, from http://www.naspa.org/kc/glbt/March2010ConventionNewsletter2.pdf.

National On-Campus Report. (2006, Jan. 15). Compromises on LGBT groups get mixed reviews. *Student Affairs Leader, 34*(2), 1, 5.

Nelson, M., and Cloyd, C. (2006, April 3). On the road: Young gay activists. *Newsweek, 147*(14). Retrieved January 5, 2011, from http://www.newsweek.com/2006/04/02/ on-the-road-young-gay-activists.html.

"New ROTC Unit Protested at University." (2008, May 9). *Baltimore Sun.* Retrieved January 4, 2011, from http://www.network54.com/Forum/233672/thread/1210352468 /1210459827/New+ROTC+Unit+Protested+at+University.

Newton, E. (2000). *Margaret Mead made me gay: Personal essays, public ideas.* Durham, NC: Duke University Press.

Nieto, S. (1996). *Affirming diversity: The sociopolitical context of multicultural education* (2nd ed.). White Plains, NY: Longman Publishers.

Nutt, A. E. (2010, October 1). Friends remember Tyler Clementi as brilliant musician, bright student. *Piscataway Star-Ledger.* Retrieved November 4, 2010, from http://www.nj.com/news/index.ssf/2010/10/rutgers_student_tyler_clementi_1.html.

Oberlin College Lambda Union. (2011). Web site. Retrieved January 2, 2011, from http://www.oberlin.edu/stuorg/lambda/.

O'Brien, K. M. (1998). The people in between: Understanding the needs of bisexual students. In R. L. Sanlo (Ed.), *Working with lesbian, gay, bisexual, and transgender college students: A handbook for faculty and administrators* (pp. 31–36). Westport, CT: Greenwood Educators Reference Collection.

Offman, C. (2005, April 16). A class apart: Transgender students at Smith College. *Financial Times.* Retrieved October 12, 2007, from http://www.howardwfrench.com/archives/2005/04/17/a_class_apart_transgender_students_at_smith_college/.

Oguntoyinbo, L. (2009, July 7). Nondiscrimination policies and support groups help ease campus life for gay and lesbian students at HBCUs. Retrieved January 11, 2011, from http://diverseeducation.com/article/12697/.

Oswalt, S. B. (2009). Don't forget the "B": Considering bisexual students and their specific health needs. *Journal of American College Health, 57*(5), 557–560.

Paley, A. (2002a). The secret court of 1920, Part I. *Harvard Crimson.* Retrieved December 5, 2010, from http://www.thecrimson.harvard.edu/article/2002/11/21/the-secret-court-of-1920-at/.

Paley, A. (2002b). The secret court of 1920, Part II. *Harvard Crimson.* Retrieved December 5, 2010, from http://www.thecrimson.com/article/2002/11/21/the-secret-court-of-1920-part-two/.

Pascarella, E. T., and Terenzini, P. T. (2005). *How college affects students. Volume 2, A third decade of research.* San Francisco: Jossey-Bass.

Patton, L. D. (2011). Perspectives on identity, disclosure, and the campus environment among African American gay and bisexual men at one historically black college. *Journal of College Student Development, 52*(1), 77–100.

Pazos, S. (1999). Practice with female-to-male transgendered youth. In G. P. Mallon (Ed.), *Social services with transgendered youth* (pp. 65–82). New York: Harrington Park Press.

Pazuniak, A. (2006, January 20). Alleged hate crime not surprising to UW. *Badger Herald.* Retrieved April 3, 2011, from http://badgerherald.com/news/2006/01/20/alleged_hate_crime_n.php.

Peirce, K. (Director). (1999). *Boys don't cry.* Hollywood: Fox Searchlight Pictures.

Perry, W. G. (1970). *Forms of intellectual and ethical development in the college years: A scheme.* Troy, MO: Holt, Rinehart and Winston.

Plaster, J. (2006). *Behind the masks: Oberlin College LGBT life from the 1920s to 1970s.* Retrieved January 2, 2011, from http://www.oberlinlgbt.org/content/Behind-the-Masks/Behind-the-Masks/behind-the-masks.html.

Pope, M. (2007). December 15, 1973: Homosexuality is delisted by the APA. In K. T. Burles (Ed.), *Great events from history: Gay, lesbian, bisexual and transgender events, 1848–2006* (pp. 265–267). Pasadena, CA: Salem Press.

Pope, R. L., and Reynolds, A. L. (1991). The complexities of diversity: Exploring multiple oppressions. *Journal of counseling and development, 70,* 174–180.

Pope, R. L., Reynolds, A. L., and Mueller, J. A. (2004*). Multicultural competence in student affairs*. San Francisco: Jossey-Bass.

Porter, J. D. (1998). Contribution of gay and lesbian identity development to transformational leadership self-efficacy. *Dissertation Abstracts International.* UMI 9836465.

Power, L. (1995). *No bath but plenty of bubbles: An oral history of the gay liberation front, 1970-3.* London: Cassell.

Poynter, K. J., and Washington, J. (2005). Multiple identities: Creating community on campus for LGBT students. In R. L. Sanlo (Ed.), *Gender identity and sexual orientation: Research, policy, and personal perspectives.* New Directions for Studet Services, No. 111. San Francisco: Jossey-Bass.

Presgraves, D. (2007, July 2). Number of gay-straight alliance registrations passes 3,500. New York: Gay, Lesbian, Straight Education Network. Retrieved January 5, 2011, from http://www.glsen.org/cgi-bin/iowa/all/news/record/2100.html.

Pusch, R. S. (2003). The bathroom and beyond: Transgendered college students' perspectives of transition. *Dissertation Abstracts International, 64*(02), 456. UMI 3081653.

Pusch, R. S. (2005). Objects of curiosity: Transgender college students' perceptions of the reactions of others. *Journal of Gay and Lesbian Issues in Education, 3*(1), 45–62.

Quart, A. (2008, March 16). When girls will be boys. *New York Times.* Retrieved January 19, 2010, from http://tinyurl.com/2l9rrp.

Rabideau, T. (2000). Finding my place in the world, or which bathroom should I use today? In K. Howard and A. Stevens (Eds.), *Out and about campus: Personal accounts by lesbian, gay, bisexual and transgendered college students* (pp. 172–180). Los Angeles: Alyson Books.

Raftery, I. (2003, Nov. 17). Can a man attend Barnard College? Transgendered students offer dilemma to Barnard College. *Columbia Spectator.* Retrieved March 27, 2007, from http://www.columbiaspectator.com/node/13402.

Rankin, S. R. (2003). *Campus climate for gay, lesbian, bisexual and transgender people: A national perspective.* New York: National Gay and Lesbian Task Force Policy Institute. Retrieved April 2, 2011, from http://www.thetaskforce.org/downloads/reports/reports /CampusClimate.pdf.

Rankin, S. R. (2004). Campus climate for lesbian, gay, and transgender people. *The Diversity factor, 12*(1), 18–23.

Rankin, S. R. (2005). Campus climates for sexual minorities. In R. Sanlo (Ed.), Gender identity and sexual orientation: Research, policy, and personal perspectives. New Directions for Student Services, No. 111. San Francisco: Jossey-Bass.

Rankin, S., and Hanson, D. (2011, March 23). LGBT campus assessments: Culture, climate, and history. *NetResults: Critical issues for student affairs practitioners.* National Association

of Student Personnel Administrators. Retrieved April 2, 2011, from http://www
.naspa.org/membership/mem/pubs/nr/default.cfm?id=1777.

Rankin, S. R., and Reason, R. D. (2008). Transformational tapestry model: A comprehensive approach to transforming campus climate. *Journal of Diversity in Higher Education, 1,* 262–274.

Rankin, S. R., Weber, G., Blumenfeld, W., and Frazer, S. (2010). *2010 state of higher education for lesbian, gay, bisexual and transgender people.* Charlotte, NC: Campus Pride.

Reed, E., Prado, G., Matsumoto, A., and Amaro, H. (2010). Alcohol and drug use and related consequences among gay, lesbian, and bisexual college students: Role of experiencing violence, feeling safe on campus, and perceived stress. *Addictive Behaviors, 35,* 168–171.

Reinhold, R. (1971, Dec. 15). Campus homosexuals organize to win community acceptance. *New York Times,* 1.

Renn, K. A. (2003). Colleges, women's. In B. Zimmerman (Ed.), *Lesbian histories and cultures: An encyclopedia* (pp. 180–182). New York: Garland.

Renn, K. A. (2007). LGBT student leaders and queer activists: Identities of lesbian, gay, bisexual, transgender and queer-identified college student leaders and activists. *Journal of College Student Development, 48*(3), 311–330.

Renn, K. A. (2010). LGBT and queer research in higher education: The state and status of the field. *Educational Researcher, 39*(2), 132–141.

Renn, K. A., and Bilodeau, B. (2005a). Leadership identity development among lesbian, gay, bisexual and transgender college leaders. *NASPA Journal, 42*(5), 342–367.

Renn, K. A., and Bilodeau, B. (2005b). Queer student leaders: An exploratory case study of identity development and LGBT student involvement at a midwestern research university. *Journal of Gay and Lesbian Issues in Education, 2*(4), 49–71.

Rhoads, R. A. (1994). *Coming out in college: The struggle for a queer identity.* Westport, CT: Bergin & Garvey.

Rhoads, R. A. (1997). A subcultural study of gay and bisexual college males: Resisting developmental implications. *Journal of Higher Education, 68*(4), 460–479.

Rhoads, R. A. (1998). *Freedom's web: Student activism in an age of cultural diversity.* Baltimore: Johns Hopkins University Press.

Rhodes, S. D., McCoy, T. P., Wilkin, A. M., and Wolfson, M. (2009). Behavioral risk disparities in a random sample of self-identifying gay and nongay male university students. *Journal of homosexuality, 56*(8), 1083–1100.

Ritchie, C. A., and Banning, J. H. (2001). Gay, lesbian, bisexual, and transgender campus support offices: A qualitative study of establishment experiences. *NASPA Journal, 38*(4), 482–494.

Ritter, K. Y., and Terndrup, A. I. (2002). *Handbook of affirmative psychotherapy with lesbians and gay men.* New York: Guilford Press.

Robin, L., and Hamner, K. (2000). Bisexuality: Identities and community. In V. A. Wall and N. J. Evans (Eds.), *Toward acceptance: Sexual orientation issues on campus* (pp. 245–260). Lanham, MD: University Press of America.

Rogers, J. (2000). Getting real at ISU: A campus transition. In K. Howard and A. Stevens (Eds.), *Out and about on campus: Personal accounts by lesbian, gay, bisexual and transgendered college students* (pp. 12–19). Los Angeles: Alyson Books.

Roper, L. (2005). The role of senior student affairs officers in supporting LGBT students: Exploring the landscape of one's life. In R. L. Sanlo (Ed.), *Gender identity and sexual orientation: Research, policy, and personal perspectives.* New Directions for Student Services, No. 111. San Francisco: Jossey-Bass.

Ropers-Huilman, B., Carwile, L., and Barnett, K. (2005). Student activists' characterizations of administrators in higher education: Perceptions of power "in the system." *Review of higher education, 28*(3), 295–312.

Ryan, R. (2005). The evolution of an LGBT center at a public institution. In R. L. Sanlo (Ed.), *Gender identity and sexual orientation: Research, policy, and personal perspectives.* New Directions for Student Services, No. 111. San Francisco: Jossey-Bass.

Sanlo, R. L. (1998). *Working with lesbian, gay, bisexual, and transgender college students: A handbook for faculty and administrators.* Westport, CT: Greenwood Educators Reference Collection.

Sanlo, R. L. (2000). The LGBT campus resource center director: The new profession in student affairs. *NASPA Journal, 37*(3), 485–495.

Sanlo, R. L. (2002). Scholarship in student affairs: Thinking outside the triangle, or Tabasco on cantaloupe. *National Association of Student Personnel Administrators Journal, 39,* 166–180.

Sanlo, R. L., Rankin, S. R., and Schoenberg, R. (2002). *Our place on campus: Lesbian, gay, bisexual, transgender services and programs in higher education.* Westport, CT: Greenwood Press.

Savin-Williams, R. C. (2001). A critique of research on sexual-minority youths. *Journal of adolescence, 24*(1), 5–13.

Savin-Williams, R. C., and Diamond, L. M. (2001). Sexual identity trajectories among sexual-minority youths: Gender comparisons. *Archives of Sexual Behavior, 29,* 419–440.

Scales, P., Leffert, N., and Lerner, R. M. (1999). *Developmental assets: A synthesis of the scientific research on adolescent development.* Minneapolis: SEARCH Institute.

Schilt, K., and Westbrook, L. (2009). Doing gender, doing heteronormativity: "Gender normals," transgender people, and the social maintenance of heterosexuality. *Gender and Society, 23*(4), 440–464.

Schlager, N. (1998). *The gay and lesbian almanac.* Detroit: St. James Press.

Schlosser, L. Z., and Sedlacek, W. E. (2001). Hate on campus: A model for evaluating, understanding, and handling critical incidents. *About Campus, 6,* 25–28.

Schnetzler, G. W., and Conant, G. K. (2009, Oct. 11). Changing genders, changing policies. *Chronicle of Higher Education.* Retrieved December 8, 2010, from http://chronicle.com/article/Changing-Genders-Changing/48733/.

Schueler, L. A., Hoffman, J. A., and Peterson, E. (2009). Fostering safe, engaging campuses for lesbian, gay, bisexual, transgender, and questioning students. In S. Harper and S. Quaye (Eds.), *Student engagement in higher education: Theoretical perspectives and practical approaches for diverse populations* (pp. 61–79). New York: Routledge.

Schumach, M. (1967, May 3). Columbia charters homosexual group. *New York Times,* p. 1.

"Settting Up an LGBT Center on Your Campus." (2006, March 15). *Student affairs leader, 34*(6), 1–2.

Silverschanz, P., Cortina, L., Konik, J., and Magley, V. (2007). Slurs, snubs, and queer jokes: Incidence and impact of heterosexist harassment in academia. *Sex Roles, 58,* 179–191.

Smith, L. (2007, March 23). Gay rights activists arrested at Oklahoma Baptist U. *Chronicle of Higher Education, 53*(29), A2.

Smothers, T. (Producer). (2006). *TransGeneration* [television series]. New York: Sundance Channel.

Sokol, D. (2003, June 24). Center of attention. *Advocate, 892,* 127–130.

Sontag, S. (1966). *Against interpretation and other essays.* New York: Farrar, Strauss & Giroux.

Soulforce. (2011). Web site. Retrieved March 3, 2011, from http://www.soulforce.org /programs/equality-ride/.

Spottiswoode, R. (Director). (2002). *The Matthew Shepard Story.* Canada: Alliance Atlantis Communications.

Steinhauer, J. (2010, Dec. 15). House votes to repeal "don't ask, don't tell." *New York Times.* Retrieved January 6, 2011, from http://www.nytimes.com/2010/12/16/us/politics /16military.html.

Stevens, R. A. (2004). Understanding gay identity development in the college environment. *Journal of College Student Development, 45*(2), 185–206.

Stoller, R. J., and others. (1973). Should homosexuality be in the APA nomenclature? *American Journal of Psychiatry, 130*(11), 1207–1216.

Strassberg, D. S., Roback, H., Cunningham, J., and Larson, P. (1979). Psychopathology in self-identified female-to-male transsexuals, homosexuals, and heterosexuals. *Archives of Sexual Behavior, 8,* 491–498.

Striegel-Moore, R. H., Tucker, N., and Hsu, J. (1990). Body image dissatisfaction and disordered eating in lesbian college students. *International Journal of Eating Disorders, 9*(5), 493–500.

Stryker, S. (2008). Transgender history, homonormativity, and disciplinarity. *Radical History Review, 100,* 145–157.

Stryker, S., and Van Buskirk, J. (1996). *Gay by the Bay: A history of queer culture in the San Francisco Bay area.* San Francisco: Chronicle Books.

"Student Homophile League Now 'Gay Liberation Front.'" (1970, Sep. 24). *Cornell Daily Sun, 87*(12), A9.

Sugano, E., Nemoto, T., and Operario, D. (2006). The impact of exposure to transphobia on HIV risk behavior in a sample of transgendered women of color in San Francisco. *AIDS and Behavior, 10,* 217–225.

Sylvia Rivera Law Project. (2011). Web site. Retrieved January 4, 2011, from http://www.srlp.org.

Tailey, A. E., Sher, K. J., and Littlefield, A. K. (2010). Sexual orientation and substance use trajectories in emerging adulthood. *Addiction, 105*(7), 1235–1245.

Talbot, D. M., and Kocarek, C. (1997). Student affairs graduate faculty members' knowledge, comfort and behaviors regarding issues of diversity. *Journal of College Student Development, 38,* 278–287.

Talbot, D. M., and Viento, W. L. (2005). *Incorporating LGBT issues into student affairs gradu-ate education.* In R. L. Sanlo (Ed.), *Gender identity and sexual orientation: Research, policy, and personal perspectives.* New Directions for Student Services, No. 111. San Francisco: Jossey-Bass.

Talburt, S. (2000). Identity politics, institutional response, and cultural negotiation: Mean-ings of a gay and lesbian office on campus. In S. Talburt and S. R. Steinberg (Eds.), *Thinking queer: Sexuality, culture and education* (pp. 60–84). New York: Peter Lang.

Teal, D. (1971). *The gay militants.* New York: Stein and Day.

Tilsley, A. (2010, June 27). New policies accommodate transgender students. *Chronicle of Higher Education.* Retrieved August 3, 2011, from http://chronicle.com/article/Colleges -Rewrite-Rules-to/66046/.

Torres, V., Jones, S. R., and Renn, K. A. (2009). Identity development theories in student affairs: Origins, current status, and new approaches. *Journal of College Student Develop-ment, 50*(6), 577–596.

Toy, J. (2008, Sep. 15). 38 years of queer liberation. *Michigan Daily.* Retrieved March 3, 2011, from http://www.michigandaily.com/content/38-years-queer-liberation.

Troiden, R. R. (1979). Becoming homosexual: A model of gay identity acquisition. *Psychia-try, 42,* 362–373.

Troiden, R. R. (1994). The formation of homosexual identities. In L. Garnets and D.C. Kimmel (Eds.), *Psychological perspectives on lesbian and gay male experiences* (pp. 191–218). New York: Columbia University Press.

U.S. Census Bureau. (2009). Current population survey: School enrollment figures. Retrieved March 1, 2011, from http://www.census.gov/population/www/socdemo /school.html.

"University profs show little interest in establishing gay course at Cornell." (1980, Nov. 21). *Cornell Daily Sun, 97*(60), 9.

Walker, D. (2007). At conservative black colleges, gays struggle to find their voice. *Associated Press.* Retrieved January 11, 2011, from http://diverseeducation.com/article/7215/.

Wall, V. A., and Evans, N. J. (2000). *Toward acceptance: Sexual orientation issues on campus.* Lanham, MD: University Press of America.

Warren, B. (2008, Jan. 29). Letter to the editor in response to the article "Gay vs. trans in America." *Advocate,* 8.

Washington, J., and Wall, V. (2006). African American gay men: Another challenge for the academy. In M. Cuyjet and Associates (Eds.), *African American men in college* (pp. 174–188). San Francisco: Jossey-Bass.

Watkins, B. L. (1998). Examining and dismantling heterosexism on college and university campuses. In R. L. Sanlo (Ed.), *Working with lesbian, gay, bisexual, and transgender college students: A handbook for faculty and administrators* (pp. 267–277). Westport, CT: Green-wood Educators Reference Collection.

Weber, L. (1998). A conceptual framework for understanding race, class, gender, and sexual-ity. *Psychology of Women Quarterly, 22(1),* 13–22.

Wehrwein, A. (1969, Nov. 25). Minn. U. recognizes club for homosexuals. *Washington Post,* A2.

Wells, A. M. (1978). *Miss Marks and Miss Woolley.* Boston: Houghton Mifflin.

Welsh, S., and Mohn, J. (2011, April 8). "Queer" is in, acronym out, AS says. *Western Washington University Western Front.* Retrieved April 10, 2011, from http://westernfrontonline .net/news/13283-queer-is-in-acronym-out-as-says.

"Wesleyan Gets Beyond Gender." (2003, June 23). *Advocate, 30.*

Westbrook, L. (2009). Where the women aren't: Gender differences in the use of LGBT resources on college campuses. *Journal of LGBT Youth, 6*(4), 369–394.

Wilchins, R. A. (2002). Queerer bodies. In J. Nestle, C. Howell, and R. A. Wilchins (Eds.), *Genderqueer: Voices from beyond the sexual binary* (pp. 33–47). Los Angeles: Alyson Books.

Wilson, A. (1996). How we find ourselves: Identity development in two-spirit people. *Harvard Educational Review, 66*(2), 303–317.

Windmeyer, S., and Freeman, P. W. (1998). *Out on fraternity row: Personal accounts of being gay in a college fraternity.* New York: Alyson Books.

Windmeyer, S. L. (2005). *Brotherhood: Gay life in college fraternities.* New York: Alyson Books.

Windmeyer, S. L. (2006). The Advocate *college guide for LGBT students: A comprehensive guide to colleges and universities with the best programs, services, and student organizations for LGBT students.* New York: Alyson Books.

Windmeyer, S. L., and Freeman, P. W. (2001). *Secret sisters: Stories of being lesbian and bisexual in college sororities.* New York: Alyson Books.

Wolf-Wendel, L. E., Toma, J. D., and Morphew, C. C. (2001). How much difference is too much difference? Perceptions of gay men and lesbians in intercollegiate athletics. *Journal of College Student Development, 42,* 465–479.

Wright, W. (2006). *Harvard's secret court: The savage 1920 purge of campus homosexuals.* New York: St. Martin's Press.

Wyss, S. (2004). "This was my hell": Violence experienced by gender nonconforming youth in U.S. high schools. *Journal of Qualitative Studies in Education, 17,* 709–730.

Yoakam, J. R. (2006). Resources for gay and bisexual students in a Catholic college. *Journal of Men's Studies, 14*(3), 311–321.

Zemsky, B. (1996). GLBT program offices: A room of our own. In B. Zimmerman and T.A.H. McNaron (Eds.), *The new lesbian studies: Into the twenty-first century.* (pp. 208–215). New York: Feminist Press.

Zemsky, B., and Sanlo, R. L. (2005). Do policies matter? In R. L. Sanlo (Ed.), *Gender identity and sexual orientation: Research, policy, and personal perspectives.* New Directions for Student Services, No. 111. San Francisco: Jossey-Bass.

Zimmerman, B. (Ed.). (2003). *Lesbian histories and cultures: An encyclopedia.* New York: Garland Publishers.

Name Index

H

Hale, D., 101
Halpin, S. A., 41
Hamner, K., 49
Hanson, D., 87
Hanson, D. E., 90
Harley, D. A., 49
Harper, S. R., 49
Harris, F., III, 49
Harris, W. G., 50
Hay, H., 17
Hayden, H. A., 57
Helms, J. E., 36
Henning-Stout, M., 69, 74
Henry, W. J., 49
Herbenick, D., 7
Highleyman, L., 20, 21
Hill, D., 68
Hirschfeld, M., 14
Hoffman, J. A., 56, 87
Holleran, A., 7
Hooker, E., 36, 37
Hoover, E., 31
Horowitz, H. L., 10
Howard, K., 8
Howard-Hamilton, M. F., 51
Hsu, J., 57
Hunter, S., 17, 82

I

Icard, L. D., 50
Inness, S. A., 11

J

Jackson, G., 11–12
James, S., 69, 74
Jay, K., 19
Johnson, C., 40
Jones, S. R., 39, 49, 51, 52, 53, 54, 55, 56, 96

K

Kafer, A., 75
Kardia, D., 18
Kasch, D., 99

Katz, J. N., 11, 12, 16, 18, 19, 27, 82
Kauffman, J. M., 40
Kellogg, A. P., 31, 56
Kerouac, J., 12
Kezar, A., 107, 108
Kimmel, D. C., 36
King, I. C., 35
King, M. L., Jr., 17
Kinsey, A., 36, 37
Kline, K. A., 99
Kocarek, C., 98, 99
Kohlberg, L., 36
Konik, J., 90
Kosciw, J. G., 8, 49, 69
Kuh, G., 98
Kulick, D., 4

L

Lark, J. S., 91, 96
Larson, P., 72
Lauritsen, J., 5
Lees, L. J., 67, 72
Leffert, N., 76
Lerner, R. M., 76
Levine, H., 31
Lewis, C. H., 36
Lipka, S., 7, 100
Littlefield, A. K., 56
Loffreda, B., 8
Loiacano, D. K., 50
Love, P. G., 31
Lowell, A. L., 14
Lynch, B., 64
Lyon, P., 17

M

McCauley, C., 26
McCoy, T. P., 57
McCray, P., 27
McEwen, M. K., 39, 52, 53, 54, 55, 56, 96
Macintosh, S., 69, 74
MacKay, A., 10, 11, 36
McKee, M., 2
McKinney, J. S., 64, 67, 74
Magley, V., 90

Savage, T. A., 49
Savin-Williams, R. C., 44, 49
Scales, P., 76
Schilt, K., 5
Schlager, N., 81, 85
Schlosser, L. Z., 71
Schnetzler, G. W., 59
Schoenberg, R., 83, 85, 87, 88, 92
Schoonmaker, C., 22
Schreiber, L., 63
Schueler, L. A., 56, 87
Schumach, M., 21
Sedlacek, W. E., 71
Shelley, M., 21
Shepard, M., 1, 8
Sher, K. J., 56
Silverchanz, P., 90
Smith, L., 31, 32
Smith, T., 74, 75
Smothers, T., 34, 63
Sokol, D., 85
Sontag, S., 13
Steinhauer, J., 33
Stevens, A., 8
Stevens, P. E., 62, 65, 66
Stevens, R. A., 49
Stoller, R. J., 37
Strassberg, D. S., 72
Striegel-Moore, R. H., 57
Stryker, S., 20, 76, 82
Sugano, E., 61

T

Tailey, A. E., 56
Talbot, D. M., 98, 99
Tarule, J. M., 36
Teal, D., 21, 22, 23
Teena, B., 8, 68
Terenzini, P. T., 98
Terndrup, A. I., 38
Thomas, M. C., 11
Tilsley, A., 32, 34, 61
Toma, J. D., 90
Torres, V., 51
Toy, J., 83
Troiden, R. R., 38, 41, 42, 43

Tubbs, N. J., 74, 75
Tucker, N., 57
Turner, M. G., 70

U

Ulrichs, K. H., 14

V

Van Buskirk, J., 82
Viento, W. L., 99

W

Walker, D., 31
Wall, V. A., 36, 48, 49, 50, 96
Walsh, P., 85
Warren, B., 95
Washington, J., 48, 50, 55, 96
Watkins, B. L., 96
Weber, G., 8, 69, 70, 89
Weber, L., 52
Wechsler, H., 56
Wehrwein, A., 22
Welsh, S., 94
Westbrook, L., 5, 94, 95
Wilchins, R. A., 67, 68
Wilcox, C., 14, 15
Wilfley, D. E., 57
Wilkin, A. M., 57
Willoughby, B., 68
Wilson, A., 51
Wilson, D., 38
Windmeyer, S., 8, 90
Wolf-Wendel, L. E., 90
Wolfson, M., 57
Woolley, M., 11
Wright, W., 15
Wyss, S., 69, 74, 90

Y

Yoakam, J. R., 93

Z

Zemsky, B., 84, 85, 95, 100
Zimmerman, B., 10

Subject Index

A

Academic homophobia: BGLT students of color and double bind of racism and, 49; directed at BGLT students, 8–9; evidence of, 15–16

Accountability: "ongoing dialogue and education" as lacking, 71; zero tolerance, 70

Activism. *See* BGLT student activism

The Advocate's guide, 90

African American gays: context-laden experiences of, 48; double bind of racism and homophobia for, 49; identity development of, 49–51; negotiating sense of their own masculinity by, 50–51

American College Health Association, 7

American College Personnel Association, 96

American Council on Education, 35

American Psychiatric Association, 37, 73

B

BGLT (bisexual, gay, lesbian, and transgender) people: Clementi's suicide as emblematic of suffering endured by, 1, 2, 3, 8, 9; history of violence against, 1–2, 8, 68–72; visibility and marginality in 20th century, 13–16; Westboro Baptist Church picketing against, 2. *See also* BGLT students

BGLT campus resource centers: campus climate assessment by, 87–90; debate over funding and visibility of, 84–85;

establishment and expansion of, 2, 81; gender gap in participation in, 94–95; higher education student affairs role in, 95–98; Lesbian-Gay Male Programs Office (University of Michigan), 82–83; narratives on genesis of the, 83–84; "new" profession of leadership at, 90–92; number of existing, 83; politics revolving around, 92–95; "Pride Center" name of Oregon State University's, 94; purposes, services, and roles of, 85–87; queer visibility movement reflected by, 81–82. *See also* Institutions

BGLT civil rights: achievements of, 33–34; activism of transgender youth in, 19–20; political terminology related to, 4; queer student activism today, 29–33; Stonewall riots (1969) heralding, 2–3, 9, 19, 102; struggle of, 1. *See also* BGLT student activism; Civil rights movement; Homophile movement

BGLT identity development: campus impediments to, 56–57; Cass's theory of homosexual, 38, 39–41; D'Augelli's life span model of, 30, 38, 44–46, 66–67; examining the 21st century context of, 47–49; Fassinger's model of, 38, 46–47; impact on student development theories by, 36–37, 110–111; intersectionality and, 51–56; reconceptualized model of multiple dimensions of identity and, 54*fig*.; of students of color, 49–51;

murder (1998) as, 1, 8; transgender students subjected to, 68–71; zero tolerance approach to, 70

Hepatitis risk, 56

HI! (City College of New York), 22

Higher education: gay culture development in pre-Stonewall, 11–12; impact on history of women by, 10–12; viewed as "breeding ground of lesbianism," 11. *See also* Institutions

Higher Education Research Institute, 29

Historically black colleges and universities (HBCUs): double marginality noted by BGLT students on, 31; studies on African American gays at, 50

History Project, 13

HIV/AIDS risk, 56

"Homonormativity," 20

Homophile movement: BGLT student role in the, 20–23; birth of the, 16–19; definition of, 5; snapshot at three institutions, 23–29. *See also* BGLT civil rights; BGLT student activism

Homophobia: BGLT students of color and double bind of racism and, 49; directed at BGLT students, 8–9; evidence of academic, 15–16. *See also* Transphobia; Violence

Homosexuality: Cass's theory of homosexual identity development, 38, 39–41; D'Augelli's life span model of identity development, 30, 38, 44–46; definition and usage of, 5; early theories advanced on, 14; Fassinger's model of BGLT identity development, 38, 46–47; perceived as "third sex," 14; Troiden's theory of homosexual identity development, 38, 41–44

Housing: activism for gender–neutral, 32; genderism of male and female separated, 68; providing suitable transgender student, 74–75

human Rights Campaign, 59

I

Identity development: core identity and, 53, 55; intersectionality used to examine, 51–56; reconceptualized model of multiple dimensions of identity and, 54*fig.*; ten common aspects of, 53. *See also* BGLT identity development; Student development theories

Institute for Sex Research, 36

Institutions: academic homophobia at, 8–9, 15–16, 49; BGLT student visibility in religiously affiliated, 31–32; genderism against transgender students in, 67–68; harassment of transgender students at, 68–71; Historically black colleges and universities (HBCUs), 31, 50; recommendations for building communities of support for transgender students, 75–78; student affairs practitioners at, 90–92, 98–99, 103–105*fig.*, 106–109; women's colleges, 10, 62–63; zero tolerance versus "ongoing dialogue and education" at, 70. *See also* BGLT campus resource centers; Campus climate assessment; Higher education

Intersectionality: BGLT identity development and role of, 51–56; insights through examining BGLT identity using, 52

Intersex, identification of, 4

Ithaca College, 28

the Ivy League, 26

L

The Ladder (monthly), 17

Lesbian–Gay Male Programs Office (University of Michigan), 82–83

Lesbians: context–laden experiences of, 48–49; higher education seen as "breeding ground" of, 11; identity development of, 37–57; impediments to healthy development in college, 56–57; students of color and identity development of, 49–51. *See also* Women

LGBT Community Center in New York, 95

Life span model: on BGLT identity development, 30, 38, 44–46; on transgender identity development, 66–67

London School of Economics, 19
Los Angeles Gay and Lesbian Center, 82

M

March to Montgomery, 18
Marxist political practices, 19
Mattachine society, 16, 17
Medical care services, 75
Mental health: campus services supporting transgender students,' 74–78; transphobia impact on, 71–72
Michigan State, 32
Mount Holyoke College, 11

N

National Association of Lesbian and Gay Community Centers, 82
National Association of Student Personnel Administrators (NASPA), 96, 97
National Center for Transgender Equality study (2011), 69
National College Health Assessment surveys, 62
National On-Campus Report (2006), 32
Native American BGLT students, 51
The New York Times, 21
New York University, 21

O

Oberlin College: D'Emilio's lecture given at, 34; LGBT history archives of, 13; Oberlin Gay Liberation (OGL) founded at, 24–25; student activism of BGLT students at, 24–25
Oberlin College Lambda Union, 25
Oberlin Gay Liberation (OGL), 24–25
Oberlin Gay Union, 25
The Oberline Review, 24
Oregon State University (OSU), 84, 94
Out and About on Campus (Howard and Stevens), 77

P

Pennsylvania State University: Homophiles of Penn State denied recognition at, 26; National Coming Out Day event at,
25–26; nondiscrimination policy instituted at, 26; queer campus resource center at, 83. *See also* University of Pennsylvania
Polyamorous, 4
Pomona College, 12
Power relations, 51–56
Praxis, 103

Q

Queer centers. See BGLT campus resource centers
Queer identity development, 38
Queer Student Cultural Center (University of Minnesota), 22
Queer theory, 99
Queers: contemporary models of identity development by, 38; context–laden experiences of students with disabilities, 49; definition and usage of, 5; impediments to healthy development in college, 56–57; visibility in religiously affiliated colleges, 31–32
Questioning identity, 4

R

Racism–homophobia double bind, 49
Religious affiliated colleges, 31–32
ROTC campus presence activism, 33
Rutgers University, 1

S

"Safe sex fatigue," 56
"Selective disclosure," 40
"Setting Up an LGBT Center on Your Campus" (2006), 92, 93, 100
Sexual Inversion (Ellis), 14
Shepard murder (1998), 1, 8
Smith College, 63
Social networking: advancing presence for queer students through, 31; BGLT student expression on, 8
Society for Human Rights, 16
Society for Individual Rights (SIR), 82
Soulforce, 32
Staff education, 74

State of Higher Education for Lesbian, Gay, Bisexual and Transgender People (Campus Pride), 89

Stigma–management strategies, 43

Stonewall riots (1969): description and significance of, 2–3, 9, 19; forces driving the, 102; homophile movement born in aftermath of, 16–19

Student affairs practitioners: BGLT campus resource center leadership by, 90–92; BGLT issues in professional preparation of, 98–99; collaborative transformation role of, 103–105*fig.*, 106–109

Student development theories: BGLT student experience impacting, 36–37, 110–111; overview of, 36. *See also* Identity development

Student Homophile League (SHL), 21–22, 27

Student personnel movement, 35–36

Students. *See* BGLT students

Swarthmore College, 32

Sylvia Rivera Law Project, 20

Syracuse University, 77

T

Teena murder, 68

Thinking Queer: Sexuality, Culture, and Education (2000), 93

"Too Queer for College" (Newton), 15

Transgender identities: cross–dresser, 60e; gender nonconforming/genderqueer, 60e; transgender, 60e; transsexual, 60e

Transgender Inclusion Committee, 96–97

Transgender students: BGLT civil rights activism of, 19–20; D'Augelli's life span model on identity development of, 66–67; description and identities of, 59–62; exacerbation of mental health effects on, 71–72; identity development of, 64–65; Internet relay chat rooms reports by, 61–62; mind–body dissonance experienced by, 65; modifying official campus documents and records on, 75; recommendations for building communities of support for,

75–78; resilience of, 72–74, 77–78; serving needs and services for, 74–78; studies on development of, 63–67; transphobia against, 62, 67–72; at women's colleges, 62–63. *See also* BGLT students; Women

Transgeneration (documentary), 63

Transphobia: exacerbation of mental health effects, 71–72; genderism, 67–68; harassment and violence of, 68–71; recommendations for institutions to fight, 76–77; transgender student's coping with, 62, 67–72. *See also* Homophobia

Transsexuals: identification with, 4; identity of, 60e

Troiden's theory of homosexual identity development, 38, 41–44

"Two Spirit," 51

U

University of Arizona, 12

University of California at Los Angeles, 34

University of California system, 32

University of Florida, 83

University of Michigan, 82–83

University of Minnesota, 22, 84, 95

University of Pennsylvania: BGLT campus resource center at, 85; campus climate assessments at, 88. *See also* Pennsylvania State University

University of South Carolina, 83

University of Wyoming, 1

U.S. Census Bureau, 66

V

Violence: Brandon Teena's murder, 68; Clementi suicide (2010), 1, 2, 3, 8, 9; exacerbation of mental health effects of, 71–72; Shepard murder (1998), 1, 8; transgender students subjected to, 68–71. *See also* Harassment; Homophobia

W

Wall Street Journal, 27

Watts riots (1965), 18
Wesleyan College, 32
Westboro Baptist Church picketing, 2
Western Washington University, 93–94
Women: gender gap in participation in
BGLT campus centers by, 94–95; impact
of higher education on history of, 10–12.

See also Lesbians; Transgender students
Women's colleges: BGLT students (late
1800s) at, 10; transgender students at,
62–63

Y

YouTube, 8

About the Author

Susan Marine is assistant professor and program director of the higher education graduate program at Merrimack College. She previously served as assistant dean of student life at Harvard College and director of the Harvard women's center; she has seventeen years of experience developing and leading initiatives in higher education for the advancement of women and gender nonconforming students, with additional expertise in student leadership development, violence prevention, and advocacy for the BGLT community. Marine conducts research in feminist praxis in higher education, transgender politics, identity, agency, the construction of alternative masculinities, and the history and future of American women's colleges. Her dissertation, *Navigating Discourses of Discomfort: Women's College Student Affairs Administrators and Transgender Students*, received a David and Myra Sadker Foundation Dissertation Award in 2009.

About the ASHE Higher Education Report Series

Since 1983, the ASHE (formerly ASHE-ERIC) Higher Education Report Series has been providing researchers, scholars, and practitioners with timely and substantive information on the critical issues facing higher education. Each monograph presents a definitive analysis of a higher education problem or issue, based on a thorough synthesis of significant literature and institutional experiences. Topics range from planning to diversity and multiculturalism, to performance indicators, to curricular innovations. The mission of the Series is to link the best of higher education research and practice to inform decision making and policy. The reports connect conventional wisdom with research and are designed to help busy individuals keep up with the higher education literature. Authors are scholars and practitioners in the academic community. Each report includes an executive summary, review of the pertinent literature, descriptions of effective educational practices, and a summary of key issues to keep in mind to improve educational policies and practice.

The Series is one of the most peer reviewed in higher education. A National Advisory Board made up of ASHE members reviews proposals. A National Review Board of ASHE scholars and practitioners reviews completed manuscripts. Six monographs are published each year and they are approximately 120 pages in length. The reports are widely disseminated through Jossey-Bass and John Wiley & Sons, and they are available online to subscribing institutions through Wiley InterScience (http://www.interscience.wiley.com).

Call for Proposals

The ASHE Higher Education Report Series is actively looking for proposals. We encourage you to contact one of the editors, Dr. Kelly Ward (kaward@wsu.edu) or Dr. Lisa Wolf-Wendel (lwolf@ku.edu), with your ideas.

Recent Titles

ORDER FORM SUBSCRIPTION AND SINGLE ISSUES

DISCOUNTED BACK ISSUES:

Use this form to receive 20% off all back issues of *ASHE Higher Education Report*.
All single issues priced at **$23.20** (normally $29.00)

TITLE   ISSUE NO.   ISBN

_____ _____ _____

_____ _____ _____

_____ _____ _____

Call 888-378-2537 or see mailing instructions below. When calling, mention the promotional code JBNND
to receive your discount. For a complete list of issues, please visit www.josseybass.com/go/aehe

SUBSCRIPTIONS: (1 YEAR, 6 ISSUES)

☐ New Order   ☐ Renewal

U.S.	☐ Individual: $174	☐ Institutional: $265
CANADA/MEXICO	☐ Individual: $174	☐ Institutional: $325
ALL OTHERS	☐ Individual: $210	☐ Institutional: $376

Call 888-378-2537 or see mailing and pricing instructions below.
Online subscriptions are available at www.onlinelibrary.wiley.com

ORDER TOTALS:

Issue / Subscription Amount: $ _____

Shipping Amount: $ _____
(for single issues only – subscription prices include shipping)

Total Amount: $ _____

SHIPPING CHARGES:

First Item $5.00
Each Add'l Item $3.00

(No sales tax for U.S. subscriptions. Canadian residents, add GST for subscription orders. Individual rate subscriptions must
be paid by personal check or credit card. Individual rate subscriptions may not be resold as library copies.)

BILLING & SHIPPING INFORMATION:

☐ **PAYMENT ENCLOSED:** *(U.S. check or money order only. All payments must be in U.S. dollars.)*

☐ **CREDIT CARD:** ☐ VISA   ☐ MC   ☐ AMEX

Card number _____ Exp. Date _____

Card Holder Name _____ Card Issue # _____

Signature _____ Day Phone _____

☐ **BILL ME:** *(U.S. institutional orders only. Purchase order required.)*

Purchase order # _____
Federal Tax ID 13559302 • GST 89102-8052

Name _____

Address _____

Phone _____ E-mail _____

Copy or detach page and send to: **John Wiley & Sons, PTSC, 5th Floor**
989 Market Street, San Francisco, CA 94103-1741

Order Form can also be faxed to: **888-481-2665**

PROMO JBNND

ENABLE
DISCOVERY

Introducing WILEY ONLINE LIBRARY

Wiley Online Library is the next-generation content platform founded on the latest technology and designed with extensive input from the global scholarly community. Wiley Online Library offers seamless integration of must-have content into a new, flexible, and easy-to-use research environment.

Featuring a streamlined interface, the new online service combines intuitive navigation, enhanced discoverability, an expanded range of functionalities, and a wide array of personalization options.

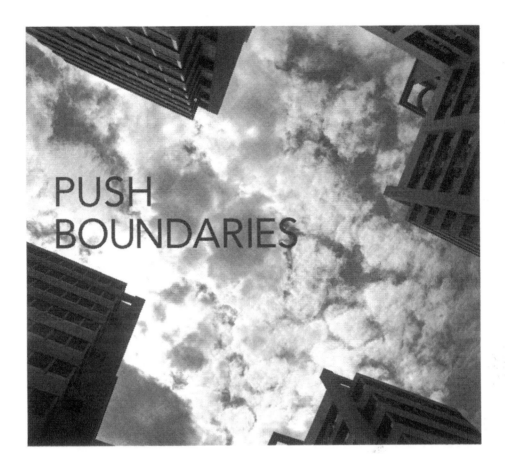